"This book is an immensely helpful guide into an inner territory that can be daunting to explore without a good guide like Michelle Van Loon. I am grateful for her wisdom and for the accessible practices she commends."

—**CHUCK DEGROAT**, author of *When Narcissism Comes to Church*, licensed therapist, and professor of pastoral care and Christian spirituality at Western Theological Seminary in Holland, Michigan

"As I grow older, I long to know more about the people in my family tree. This timely book helps me reconcile the people and places that make up my genealogy. *Translating Your Past* is a gift box for every reader, reminding us that our story is a valuable mosaic, carefully woven together by the Author of life. Michelle Van Loon's words welcome us to behold our beautiful and broken family history through a redemptive lens, assuring us that we are indeed part of God's good work!"

—**DORENA WILLIAMSON**, bestselling author of *ColorFull* and *The Celebration Place*

"Michelle Van Loon weaves together the stories of biblical characters, modern men and women, and her own family to help us map the blessings and curses of our past and make sense of our family stories. A wise, redemptive, fascinating book for everyone interested in family history, intergenerational wounds, and the possibility for healing."

—**AMY JULIA BECKER**, author of *A Good and Perfect Gift* and the forthcoming *To Be Made Well*

"Not long ago, an unknown and unexpected relative came into our lives thanks to genetic testing. No one quite knew what to do, and this kind of surprise is becoming more common. How do we come to terms with surprises? With secrets? With family trauma? How do we reconcile both the coexisting goodness and darkness of our family histories? 'God will use the voices of our past in our present,' writes Michelle Van Loon in her wise and informed book, *Translating Your Past*. Thanks to this book, I'm learning to listen."

—**SUSAN FLORY**, *New York Times* bestselling author and coauthor, writer's conference director, and founder of Everything Memoir

"As a therapist and former history teacher, I'm elated by the content of this book. We humans are products of our stories, of the family systems into which we are born, and of the genetic code handed down to us. When we understand who we are and the family and cultural environments in which we are socialized, we are better able to understand ourselves and heal from various wounds. Michelle Van Loon guides the reader to see how our family stories provide insight into both our struggles and joys. I highly recommend this resource!"

—**BRENDA YODER**, licensed mental health counselor, educator, and author of *Fledge: Launching Your Kids without Losing Your Mind*

"*Translating Your Past* is an important work that invites all of us to step into our past to bring healing into our present and to transform our future. These steps affect those around us and those yet to come. Each chapter provides necessary threads to help us face and process the array of factors that form our identity: family history, genetics, generational patterns, ethnicity, religion, plus maneuvering the unknowns, adoption, and trauma. The biblical story frames and undergirds the dialogue. A recommended read for everyone looking to be more whole."

—**INGRID FARO**, PhD, MDiv, visiting professor of Old Testament at Northern Seminary

"Families don't come with a gift receipt. We can't return the bad back we got from Grandpa or the receding hairline we got from Grandma. Our family inheritance, like the Star Wars series, is going to have stories we are proud of and stories we wish were never created (like Episodes 1–3). In Michelle Van Loon's latest book, *Translating Your Past*, she teaches us how to learn from the past, live in the present, and look forward to the future. Thanks to this book I'm hoping to set aside more money for my kids' college tuition and less for their future therapy sessions."

—**DAN STANFORD**, author of *Losing the Cape: The Power of Ordinary in a World of Superheroes*

"In *Translating Your Past*, Michelle Van Loon helps readers unwrap the threads of the past and better understand how genetics, ancestry, and trauma influence the patterns we weave into our present and future. This book provides a much-needed tool that assists readers in recognizing the many factors that contribute to attitudes, health, personality, and character strengths, and the author writes with grace and insightful narrative that draw the reader from page to page. *Translating Your Past* is a vital book for psychologists, social workers, educators, the medical community, people helpers, families, clergy, and the faith community. It combines cutting-edge research, spiritual application, and practical resources for anyone looking for help understanding the critical role of our past in shaping our present and future. A must-read for anyone who wants to better understand themselves and others."

—**SHELLY BEACH**, cofounder of PTSD Perspectives and coauthor of the award-winning *Love Letters from the Edge: Meditations for Those Struggling with Brokenness, Trauma, and the Pain of Life*

"Michelle Van Loon's intriguing compilation of life stories and biblical wisdom, in conversation with psychosocial and biological theories, invites people from multiple familial backgrounds and configurations to discover deeper understanding and healing for complex inherited patterns, joys, and challenges. Van Loon's findings through this thoughtful, integrative work are accessible and readily applicable through the questions, suggestions, and resources generously recommended throughout the book. A timely gift!"

—**MARY THIESSEN NATION**, affiliate professor at Eastern Mennonite Seminary

Translating Your Past

FINDING MEANING IN
FAMILY ANCESTRY,
GENETIC CLUES, AND
GENERATIONAL TRAUMA

Michelle Van Loon

HERALD PRESS

Harrisonburg, Virginia

Herald Press
PO Box 866, Harrisonburg, Virginia 22803
www.HeraldPress.com

Library of Congress Cataloging-in-Publication Data
Names: Van Loon, Michelle, author.
Title: Translating your past : finding meaning in family ancestry, genetic clues, and
    generational trauma / Michelle Van Loon.
Other titles: Finding meaning in family ancestry, genetic clues, and generational
    trauma
Description: Harrisonburg, Virginia : Herald Press, [2022] | Includes
    bibliographical references.
Identifiers: LCCN 2021050980 (print) | LCCN 2021050981 (ebook) |
    ISBN 9781513809519 (paperback) | ISBN 9781513809526 (hardcover) |
    ISBN 9781513809496 (ebook)
Subjects: LCSH: Genealogy—Religious aspects. | DNA—Social aspects. |
    Intergenerational relations—Psychological aspects. | BISAC: RELIGION /
    Christian Living / Personal Growth | FAMILY & RELATIONSHIPS / General
Classification: LCC CS16 .V36 2022 (print) | LCC CS16 (ebook) | DDC
    929.1—dc23
LC record available at https://lccn.loc.gov/2021050980
LC ebook record available at https://lccn.loc.gov/2021050981

Study guides are available for many Herald Press titles at
www.HeraldPress.com.

TRANSLATING YOUR PAST
© 2022 by Herald Press, Harrisonburg, Virginia 22803. 800-245-7894.
    All rights reserved.
Library of Congress Control Number: 2021050980
International Standard Book Number: 978-1-5138-0951-9 (paperback);
    978-1-5138-0952-6 (hardcover); 978-1-5138-0949-6 (ebook)
Printed in United States of America
Cover and interior design by Merrill Miller
Cover photo by Daisy-Daisy/iStockphoto/Getty Images

All scripture quotations, unless otherwise indicated, are taken from the *Holy
Bible, New International Version*®, NIV®. Copyright ©1973, 1978, 1984, 2011 by
Biblica, Inc.™ Used by permission of Zondervan. All rights reserved worldwide.
www.zondervan.com. The "NIV" and "New International Version" are trademarks
registered in the United States Patent and Trademark Office by Biblica, Inc.™

All scripture marked with the designation "GW" is taken from *GOD'S WORD*®.
© 1995, 2003, 2013, 2014, 2019, 2020 by God's Word to the Nations Mission Society.
Used by permission.

Scripture quotations marked "*The Message*" are taken from THE MESSAGE,
copyright © 1993, 2002, 2018 by Eugene H. Peterson. Used by permission of Nav-
Press, represented by Tyndale House Publishers. All rights reserved.

26 25 24 23 22   10 9 8 7 6 5 4 3 2 1

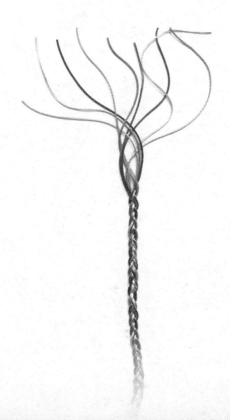

"One generation commends your works to another;
they tell of your mighty acts."
—Psalm 145:4

Contents

Foreword

I COME FROM A LONG LINE of stubborn Germans. As one relative of mine likes to say, "You can always tell a German, you just can't tell them very much." Some of my family stories are hilarious or legendary—I once walked miles out of my way in subzero temperatures without a jacket because, despite my husband's gentle protestations, I was *so certain I knew the directions*—while others are profoundly tragic. I carry each of them in my psyche and in my bones.

As part of my ministerial training, I created a family genogram. This assignment required me to compile not just my family tree but details about each of the people in its branches. After conversations with both sets of grandparents, it began to dawn on me that I was not simply an independent actor on the stage of life. Instead, I was the product of genetics, family culture, and a sizable cast of characters rife with both glory and shame.

The same is true for each of us. Scripture tells us that we are not our own, and perhaps nowhere is that as evident as when we begin digging into our family histories, where we inevitably learn that the tapestries of our lives include both bright threads and ragged ones leading back generations.

While we may be tempted to believe that what's come before us is forever behind us, in this book Michelle Van Loon wisely notes, "What is essential to the translator's task is an awareness of the gravitational pull that generational patterns and consequences may have in our lives." The work of making sense of our past is critical not only for us as individuals, but also for the communities in which we live and serve and for the generations that will follow us.

Van Loon wisely guides us to consider how we might begin setting down burdens we may not even have known we were carrying. As we take a fearless inventory of our generational stories and begin to heal from buried pain, we will also find new delight in discovering God's faithfulness at work even before our birth. She writes, "Faithful translators . . . will be as unflinching in our assessment of the goodness in our stories as we are in capturing the sorrows."

Translating Your Past takes us on an exciting journey, but also a perilous one. Uncovering family secrets can be disruptive, people we love may express anger that we aren't "letting sleeping dogs lie," and we may even discover painful realities that transform our understanding of ourselves and our histories.

Yet we serve a God of unchanging truth. Here Van Loon masterfully engages with the biblical story of sins that trickle down from parents to children to grandchildren, but also of God's faithfulness shown to a thousand generations of those who love and follow God.

Translating Your Past is a gentle invitation into the hard work of growth and the free gift of God's grace. Its core invitation is clear: unless we understand where we've come from, we will forever walk with a rock in our shoe, limping without knowing why.

I don't know about you, but I don't want a rock in my shoe. (I also don't want to walk freezing miles without a jacket anymore, because with Van Loon's help—and good friends, good therapists, and lots of Jesus!—even a stubborn German from a long line of stubborn Germans can learn some gracious humility.)

Let's sit with Van Loon's wise words and the Lord and shake out that shoe.

It's time to dance.

—Courtney Ellis, author of *Happy Now: Let Playfulness Lift Your Load and Renew Your Spirit*

Introduction

THE PAST IS SPEAKING. But many of us hear only the sounds of static and gibberish.

We may believe we're passably fluent in the vocabulary of the present. William Shakespeare wrote, "What's past is prologue; what to come / in yours and my discharge."[1]

Our family stories are our prologue.

In our hands—at our discharge, as the Bard would say—are the tools we can use to translate the complex "languages" of ancestry, genetics, and trauma that create our unique prologue. Learning to interpret our family history will help us better understand who we are and guide us toward discovering our place in our family, church, and world.

If you visit a self-help section in a bookstore, you'll find a variety of attractive blueprints for how to build a strong family, a happy marriage, and a winning life. Some churches offer congregants spiritualized versions of these plans. But the building materials that God gives each one of us to use come in part through our one-of-a-kind family stories that include history, DNA, trauma, consequences of ancestors' choices, mysteries, adoption, race, ethnicity, religious tradition, and more. Those components will never fit neatly into someone else's one-size-fits-all building plan.

To think of it another way, imagine that someone dumped the contents of ten three-thousand-piece vintage puzzles each featuring the artwork of various French impressionists onto the floor. Out of that colorful chaos, you are invited to put the pieces of the puzzles together to create an entirely new three-dimensional sculpture. How do you make sense of all those complex pastel puzzle pieces? If each of those pieces represents a distinctive bit of your family history, how can you begin to figure out how they fit together? Does the task call for artistry in creating something new, or a good set of detective skills to sift through the cacophony of puzzle pieces scattered all over the floor? How can you interpret the various elements that went into producing your prologue?

We'll address these questions as we explore together how to approach translation of our stories so we can find a deeper connection to God and the world around us, gain a fuller understanding of those who came before us, and discover the necessary tools to be able to pass on a rich and hopeful legacy to those who may come after us.

Translation is both art and science. Not long ago, I saw a picture of a restaurant menu highlighting an entrée called "Chicken Rude and Unreasonable." My family once raised backyard poultry, and I can confirm that chickens can be quite sassy. However, it appeared that the foreign-born restaurateur wasn't offering a commentary on obnoxious roosters and hens but had used Google Translate so he could let his customers know he was adding a Caribbean-style jerk chicken dish to his menu.

A translator converts words from one language into words in another language. The technical side of a translator's role includes a mastery of grammar and vocabulary of both languages. The art involved in translation includes nimble interpretation of each language's nuances, idioms, and slang. Language is a living, ever-evolving thing, and sensitivity to how real people communicate is the difference between a skilled human translator and a computer program that might get the words correct but obscure the meaning in the process.

Translation expert Bijay Kumar Das writes, "A translator is a reader, an interpreter and a creator all in one."[2] As we seek to make sense of the story of our ancestry, genes, and generational trauma of the past, we are engaging in a sacred call to listen, understand, and transmit meaning. Some might view the subject of exploring family stories as a self-indulgent exercise in nostalgia, but if a cache of wistful, melancholy, sepia-toned memories is the sole product of this effort, then we are missing the profound gifts of identity, purpose, and hope that come with the redemptive work of translating the past.

For the Christian, it is not a novel idea that we are always in conversation with the past (see, e.g., Deuteronomy 6:4–9; Psalm 71:18; Proverbs 1:7; 2 Timothy 1:5). The Bible describes how God uses beloved and imperfect humans to communicate faith from one generation to the next. Scripture's unflinching account can strengthen us as we listen to the sometimes complicated and confusing messages our story may be telling us and can help us interpret them with clarity and grace. That kind of interpretation is the essence of the translator's task.

Learning to love the face in the mirror

We may think about specific aspects of our family stories if we land in a counselor's chair, a doctor's office, or bake Grandma's legacy fruitcake recipe every Christmas (even if no one eats it except for Great-Uncle Edgar). But each time we connect what may seem at first to be disconnected puzzle pieces, we are moving toward wholeness and growing in understanding of who we are and who God is.

After our mom died in 2007, my younger sister and I found a stash of old photo albums that our father had created before his death ten years earlier. There were some wonderful images of our childhoods and older snapshots of our parents' wedding. As we leafed through the pages of other old albums, we saw black-and-white snapshots that captured the joy and struggle of the early years of my father's immigrant parents in the United States: our paternal grandmother, wrapped in a forty-eight-star American flag shortly after her arrival in this country in 1914; a picture of my paternal grandfather's American dream—his very own junkyard in Peoria, Illinois; gatherings with other relatives who'd made it out of Eastern Europe around the same time they had.

In one of those old photo albums, my sister and I discovered a series of pictures of our mother we'd never seen before. Until that moment, I realized I'd never seen a single snapshot of my mother as a baby, child, or young teen. She was born to Eastern European Jewish immigrants, just as our father was. My sister and I had always known that like many young Jewish women of her generation in the years after World War

II, our mother had gotten a rhinoplasty, more commonly known as a nose job, when she was in her teens in order to reduce the size of her nose so she wouldn't look so "ethnic." Her goal was to better fit in with modern American ideals of beauty. Then, because she was still unhappy with the results of the first surgery, she underwent a second rhinoplasty to further reduce the size of her nose. Until the day my sister and I found that album, the only picture I'd ever seen of my mother before she met my father was her high school graduation picture, which was taken after her second surgery.

Seeing photographs of my mother as a child was like looking into a mirror. I looked just like her. And those images brought something else into focus for me. When I was a child, my mom often told me how unattractive I was, followed by a pledge that when I was old enough, my parents would make sure I would have a nose job to "fix" my damaged appearance.

In fact, I'd had a consultation with a Chicago surgeon when I was fifteen, and my parents scheduled the procedure right after I finished my school year. But a few months earlier, I'd come to faith in Jesus the Messiah. As a result, I was rethinking whether I really needed to undergo the surgery. Was it possible that God loved me just as I was? Though that truth felt more like a wish than a settled reality at that point in my life, in faith I elected to cancel the procedure. My parents never said a word about it again.

When I saw those pictures of my mother as a child, I realized that she had seen her younger self in the mirror of my childhood face.

Some puzzle pieces clicked together for me in that moment that connected to other discoveries I'd been making through the years about my family story. This side of heaven, we will never be able to put together every puzzle piece we are given in our lives. But as we engage in the ongoing work of translating the past, we will find ourselves growing toward spiritual wholeness and maturity, free to love God and neighbor as we are learning to love ourselves.

In these pages . . .

This book will give you a thoughtful overview of the key elements that contribute to our family stories. Each chapter will explore a different theme, combining contemporary research, fascinating personal accounts, and relevant insights from the Bible:

- Learning to pay attention to the story the past is telling us

- Anchoring ourselves in a larger story as we delve into our own family history

- Deciphering the language of our DNA

- Understanding how trauma can encode itself into our family history

- Identifying the consequences of our forebears' decisions

- Listening to the mysteries in our family narrative

- Discovering the blessings and challenges of adoption in a family's story

- Discerning how race, ethnicity, and religion shaped the experience and identity of our ancestors

- Seeing how interpreting the past gives meaning to our

present and helps us create an informed, faithful legacy for the future

The stories I share throughout this book are true, though I've changed names and identifying details at the request of some of the individuals who generously shared their experiences with me.

Each chapter concludes with a set of reflection questions you can use for personal journaling or to spark lively discussion with your small group, book club, or Bible study. Appendix A offers tools you can use to capture the various threads of your own family story. The prompts in this section can clarify what you already know about your story and can help launch you into areas you may wish to research further. If you're hoping to create a written account of your family history to pass on to the next generation, this section will assist you in that task. Finally, Appendix B contains a list of additional readings and resources if you're looking to take a deeper dive into a particular topic covered in these pages.

The past is speaking. Lord, give us ears to hear.

ONE

Message in a Bottle

Learning to Pay Attention to the Story the Past Is Telling Us

ON'T YOU EVER WONDER where you come from?"
I knew I was breaking an unwritten rule in my family by asking my mom that question. That rule had suffocated every discussion of family history for as long as I could remember. Though I knew the skeleton story of my mom's origins, I learned early that if no one asked any questions, there'd be no need to reckon with the painful answers.

The ice-cold fire in my mom's eyes told me I had crossed a line. "No," she answered, and paused a moment before she turned her back to me to signal that the discussion was over. But before she did, I thought I saw something different steal across her face—something I'd never witnessed before. I saw deep sadness, just for a moment, before her anger locked it away where no one could get near it.

I was very familiar with that anger. But I'd never seen the sadness before.

I had been emboldened to break the rule by the cultural moment in which we were living. The groundbreaking 1977 television miniseries based on author Alex Haley's bestselling book *Roots: The Saga of an American Family*, which details his quest to trace his family's lineage through generations of inhumane slavery in the South back to their homeland in Gambia, had ignited a wave of popular interest in genealogy.

Before the modern civil rights movement, genealogical research tended to be reserved for royalty and for those looking to establish their pedigree to belong in socially and racially exclusive organizations like the Daughters of the American Revolution.[1] The *Roots* miniseries shattered those notions for many viewers, who found in Haley's saga the encouragement they needed to discover and honor their own family stories for the first time.

Professional genealogist Juliana Szucs notes, "The impact of *Roots* transformed family history at local and national levels. Previously, there had been a perception that family history could only be done by the elite few who could afford to travel or pay professionals to conduct research on their behalf. Alex Haley's experience tracing his African American family history using many records found at the National Archives and oral interviews made it clear that it was possible for almost everyone to discover their own family story."[2]

My hunger to know about the missing pieces of my family's story gave my teenage self a boost of boldness as I decided to press my mother that day in 1977 in our suburban Chicago kitchen. I took a deep breath and forged ahead. "You might not want to know, but I do, Mom." She kept her back turned to me, and her silence signaled that the conversation was over.

Sometimes our family stories are a book we'd rather not open.

Even when we might wish to leave that book on the shelf, we bear those stories deep within us. We carry with us genetic code, the history of the family in which we grew up, the influence of the communities and culture that both formed our forebears and shapes our own life experience, and the unique imprint of our Maker who created us. Our history is not destiny, but it is a living preface to our experience.

But many of our stories are anything but easy reading. Some have sections written in indecipherable text or appear to be missing chapters. Others appear stitched together from a variety of unrelated volumes or have shredded pages. These accounts have been written by many authors, in many places and times, and often seem more like a bunch of faded, illegible messages in multiple bottles that have washed up on a distant shore—a curiosity, but with nothing meaningful to say to us here and now.

We may consider leaving family stories unexplored for lots of other reasons, including

- *Dysfunction:* Veering wide from a family history filled with abuse, addiction, or neglect may indeed be a necessary healthy coping mechanism. Why go there when the past is filled with such pain?

- *Death:* The knowledge and firsthand experience of our parents and grandparents is buried when earlier generations die. This is amplified for those whose forbears survived genocide or war and lost many members of their extended families. Why bother searching for what is gone forever?

- *Disconnection:* In our highly mobile society, families scatter and lose connection. The bonds simply couldn't be sustained. Why invest in relationships that have naturally faded away?

- *Complexity:* This is best illustrated by the challenges faced by "third culture" kids—those who have grown up in a culture different from the national origins of both parents. When there are many stories to consider, which narrative or narratives and in what proportion can best define a person's identity?

- *Confusion:* The subject seems daunting. How can a person begin to make sense of the jumble of messages in bottles sent from the past? What if there is no record of the past to explore?

- *Fear:* What bad surprises might be lurking in the past? Isn't it better to just let the proverbial sleeping dogs lie?

- *Devaluing the past:* How does spending time looking in history's rearview mirror help us right now? It's just a bunch of dusty museum curiosities, right?

- *The urgency of daily life:* Considering the past is a pursuit reserved for the privileged. Those simply trying to survive day to day have more important things to think about. Why devote energy to something that can't put food on the table?

These are fair concerns. However, even in the busyness of daily life, our soul is always searching for the answer to larger existential questions: "Who am I?" and "Why am I here?" Our family stories can provide important information that can guide us as we seek to answer those questions.

Philosopher and poet Ralph Waldo Emerson said, "Every man is a quotation from all his ancestors."[3] Just as punctuation marks insert rhythms and necessary pauses into a string of words, so the gaps and silences in our stories add meaning to the pieces of our history that we are able to access. It may seem counterintuitive, but the truth is that even the confusing or chaotic chapters in our family history can add clarity to our understanding of our identity. That said, some readers may find that raw areas of grief and pain in their family story call for processing in the companionship of a counselor, trusted pastor, spiritual director, or wise friend.

But even when it is a challenge, the process of remembering can inform the way we begin to answer those essential questions about our existence. Bible readers find throughout Scripture a call to "remember well" that can guide us as we begin to translate our family's past.

For instance, amid one of the series of crises that marked his life, King David pled for God's help. An integral part of his cry for help was his intention to remember: "I *remember* the days of long ago; I *meditate* on all your works and *consider* what your hands have done." (Psalm 143:5, italics mine). The visceral verbs used in this verse are instructive as to why this kind of remembering was essential to David's present-tense experience. "Remember" is the translation of the Hebrew word *zakar*, which describes experiencing a past event as if it were happening right now. The word "meditate" is the translation of the word *hagah*, which means "to growl and groan." *Siyach*, which means "consider," carries with it the notion of complaining as well as meditating. David understood what it meant to remember as something like being immersed in an intense flashback intended to catalyze him in the present toward both meaningful action and deeper devotion.

The New Testament picks up the thread of active remembrance with the genealogies connecting Jesus to his forebears in the Old Testament (Matthew 1:1–18; Luke 3:23–38). The woman standing at the hinge of history, Mary, responded to the news that she would give birth to God's Son with a song of praise found in Luke 1:46–55. Her words of remembrance connect her life to the story that God had been writing in the lives of previous generations of her family:

> His mercy extends to those who fear him,
> *from generation to generation.* . . .
> He has helped his servant Israel,
> *remembering to be merciful*
> to Abraham and his descendants forever,
> *just as he promised our ancestors.*
> (Luke 1:50, 54–55, italics mine)

Jesus orients our remembrance Godward as well as toward one another. The word *remembrance* (*anamnesis*) was used by Jesus as he instituted the practice of communion during the final Passover meal he shared with his disciples. When he passed the cup and unleavened bread to them, he told them to remember him together every time they partook, and Paul repeated the instruction in his letter to the Corinthian church

(Luke 22:18–20; 1 Corinthians 11:23–25). *Anamnesis*, like the Hebrew *zakar*, points to an active, participatory experience of remembrance.

Remembering God well is dramatically different from recalling information about what God has done, as if we were prepping for a Sunday school Bible quiz. Remembering our story well is not an invitation to enjoy a personalized family fairy tale. Instead, remembering well is active, ongoing engagement with the Author of our story.

The Bible tells us we are made in the image of God (Genesis 1:27). God creates us from the genes of our biological parents; forms us within the family among whom we're raised; refines us through the people, places, and times in which we live; and welcomes us into God's family through faith. God has used a brand-new combination of each of those things for every human being who has ever lived to reflect something unique of God's eternal glory. Though contemporary Western culture has trained us to view ourselves primarily as individuals, this emphasis diminishes the reality that we are built for relationship via family and community, and that we are inextricably connected to those who came before us as well as those who will come after us.

Welcoming the cast of the past

Many other world cultures place a high value on family stories. For example, in some Buddhist cultures, recorded clan histories called *jiapu* (pronounced chia-poo) or *zupu* (dzoo-poo), sometimes going back hundreds of years or more, are treasured artifacts. As one Chinese family tree researcher explains, "It is important to remember that *zupu* were written by clans to glorify their ancestors—so its contents must be taken with a pinch of salt and should be treated as any other compiled family history source. Compilers were often selective about what and who they included in the zupu: individuals who disgraced the family were typically not mentioned, and seeing as the clan was a heavily patrilineal institution, only scant details were kept of wives, sisters and daughters."[4]

Jiapu and zupu were connected to the Buddhist practice of ancestor veneration, but the high value the clan placed on their shared history also contributed to members' understanding of their identity. In China, many of these ancient documents were destroyed during the Cultural Revolution that took place from 1966 to 1976. However, numerous other jiapu/zupu were preserved by being hidden or shipped overseas. During the past twenty to thirty years, there has been a resurging interest in southern China in re-creating clan and family histories.[5]

Rev. Bernard Smith, an American-born seminary professor who has been living in the West African country of Togo for more than two decades, told me that most African cultures have a deep tradition of honoring their elders and teaching their children their oral genealogies. "A few years ago," he said, "I admitted to one of my students that I didn't know the name of my great-grandfather. He looked confused and said, 'If I didn't already know your character, I would have called you a liar! I have no idea how someone can live without that knowledge.'" Many African clans have an appointed storyteller charged with passing on the tribe's history and traditions, including the names of ancestors going back as many as thirty generations.[6]

Family history shapes our understanding of who we are, no matter where in the world we live. "Our stories help us make sense of our lives, give us hope that we will sustain and overcome, and help us predict a better future," says psychologist Robyn Fivush.[7] Fivush and fellow psychologist Marshall Duke created a twenty-question tool called "Do You Know?" that asked children to answer questions like, "Do you know some things that happened to your mom or dad when they were in high school?"; "Do you know where some of your grandparents grew up?"; and "Do you know the source of your name?" They analyzed the results along with additional psychological testing done on the children and discovered that in comparison to children who didn't know much about their family's story, the children who knew details about the experiences of their parents and grandparents tended to have higher self-esteem and expressed the belief that their families were connected in meaningful ways.[8] Fivush notes, "It is not the knowledge of these specific facts that is important—it is the process of families sharing stories about their lives that is important."[9]

Family stories pass on resilience, empathy, and self-acceptance. Writer Mary Quigley suggests that stories of regret and failure are as essential as the stories of heroes and wins in a family: "While the peaks of a family history are important, so are the valleys; there are lessons to be learned from failure." She points toward a family story research study that asked students to talk about a time when their parents did something wrong, noting, "We thought we'd get rule-breaking and similar stories, but we also got a lot of stories of regrets: regrets about not going to a certain college or not working hard enough when they were younger."[10]

God is in the redemption business and can redeem even our deepest regrets.[11] Passing on those stories builds empathy and understanding for those who came before us—another way that we can engage in interpreting the choices of our forebears so we can make meaning of them as a gift to the next generation in our family story.

When I asked my mom about her origins, I knew at least some of the answers to my questions were only a phone call away. I grew up knowing some basic facts about her story: Her mother, my maternal grandmother Molly Klopman, died shortly after giving birth to my mom in 1938 in New York City. Her father George wasn't able to care for a newborn. An infertile cousin and her husband in Chicago agreed to adopt the baby with the proviso that the adoption remain a secret. Everyone in the family agreed it would be for the best. But shortly before my mother was to marry, George called and spilled the truth in 1957. He wanted to come to the wedding to see Molly's baby walk down the aisle.

That information was a grenade that blew up my mom's life, though no one in the family understood at the time just how deep the damage went. Instead, the shrapnel was reconfigured in time for happy family pictures with the parents who'd raised her. I've been told that George came to the wedding and sat in the back of the room. He's not in any of the pictures in the wedding album.

I would discover that beneath this sketch of the facts, there was a pile of pain around these secrets that my mom didn't want to touch and couldn't forgive. I may not have had words for it at the time, but when I asked my mom for more information about her family of origin in 1977, I was looking for the truth about not only her life, but mine.

As we translate our past, we can discover in the company of our heavenly Father that his truth can set us free in the present in ways we never imagined.

Reflect

1. What areas of resistance, if any, do you have to the idea of delving into the stories of your family?

2. What question do you most wish you could ask a deceased forebear? Why?

3. As you consider Mary's words in Luke 1:46–55, why do you think it is significant that the mother of Jesus makes mention of the generations who came before her, those who were alive at the time she sang this prayer, and those, like us, who would come after her?

TWO

〜

The Original Family Tree

Anchoring Ourselves in a Larger Story as We Delve into Our Own Family History

ARLY CHURCH FATHER Augustine of Hippo is often quoted as saying, "The Holy Scriptures are our letters from home." These letters from home capture the complexity of family life as well as the loving and fair character of the family's Head. Scripture's narrative can reorient us as we navigate complex and confusing elements of our own unique history while simultaneously anchoring us in God's grand story.

When we think about the opening pages of the very first letter from home, a tree containing forbidden fruit is spotlighted in the drama between a Man, a Woman, a Liar, and their Creator that unfolds in the garden of Eden. But God planted another kind of tree in that garden. It was the genesis of humankind's family tree, birthed in the lives of Adam and Eve. The root of the human tree was transplanted from the garden into a harsher environment, a consequence of the disobedient decisions the first couple made in response to God's gracious instructions to them.

Once Adam and Eve were outside the perfect shalom of the garden, the Bible tells us that the pair's intimacy resulted in two children, Cain and Abel. This first branch of the family tree introduced the element of weapons-grade sibling rivalry that resulted in Cain murdering his brother. God preserved Cain's life, but echoing the pattern of his parents, Cain lived out the consequences of his action as he was sent far from the only home he'd known into exile as "a restless wanderer" (Genesis 4:12).

Genesis 4 hints at the way Cain's earthly days were shadowed by those consequences: He had to face potential enemies who might seek to cause him harm and was responsible for the protection of a wife who had traveled into the harsh unknown with him. We learn that at some point in his wilderness wandering, Cain created an encampment for his children and grandchildren. Genesis 4:17–24 cites a variety of skill sets his descendants developed in that village-city, including shepherding livestock, building musical instruments, and forging tools. Though Cain was banished for committing murder, the fruitfulness of his family's life in the wilderness suggests he maintained and passed on to subsequent generations a connection with his Creator and Savior.

Meanwhile, bereft of both children, Adam and Eve introduced another son, Seth, to the story. Genesis 5 shifts the focus back to this branch of the family tree, sketching for us a progression of generations from Seth to Noah. It is helpful for data-driven moderns like us to remember that the focus of ancient genealogies was to establish ancestry, rather than to create a detailed historical record. Genealogies in Scripture had one or more of three distinct purposes:

- *Domestic genealogies* focused on the privileges and inheritance rights of firstborn sons.

- *Legal genealogies* focused on detailing bloodlines for those claiming governmental roles, military commissions, or deeded land.

- *Religious genealogies* focused on ensuring that only those from God-appointed family groups would serve in designated priestly roles.[1]

We find in Genesis 10 an example of a wide-ranging domestic genealogy, as seventy names are listed as the direct descendants of Noah's three sons.[2] These names represent the repopulation of the earth into tribal people groups after the catastrophic flood. Later, on the plain of Shinar, Genesis 11 records the scattering and exile of these clans from one another, a consequence of their arrogant plan to build themselves a tower so they could guarantee themselves security in an often bewildering world.

Number the stars

The letters from home then shift their focus to an infertile, aging couple living in what is now Iraq. The couple's age and childlessness meant this branch on the family tree of a man named Terah had become a fruitless dead end.

God sent an unprecedented direct message to seventy-five-year-old Abram. It included the command to leave home and family and travel to a place that would be revealed as he journeyed. God also gave Abram a set of impossible-sounding promises about becoming the father of a great nation who'd be a blessing to every family scattered around the world (Genesis 12:1–3; 17:1–14).

Abram said yes with his life by leaving his home and family in Ur and stepping into the unknown with his wife, nephew, and some servants and livestock. As he wandered, sometimes stumbling along the way, he continued to grow in his knowledge of God. Abram's initial zigzag journey from Iraq to Egypt and back to the land of Canaan turned into a decade-long sojourn. The old man had become an even older man, and Abram began making plans to distribute his estate. Under the rules of the prevailing culture, his possessions would have gone to his faithful servant Eliezer.

At this point, God again repeated the promise that Abram would have progeny as numerous as the stars in the sky, along with an asterisk that a day would come when Abram's descendants would become slaves for four centuries. God sealed the covenant with a sacrifice that God himself provided (Genesis 15). After living in Canaan for ten years, Abram then attempted to bring this promise to pass by pressing one of the slaves, Hagar, into service of this promise.[3]

An epic level of strife between Abram's longtime wife Sarai and Hagar erupted when Hagar became pregnant. Hagar fled into the wilderness, seemingly without much of a plan other than not to be anywhere near Sarai. A messenger sent from God appeared to Hagar as she sat along a small spring in the wilderness, telling her that this child would be enfolded in the blessing given to Abram of descendants too numerous to count. The messenger also gave her a heads-up that her baby would be a wild child in this world. Abram became a first-time father at age eighty-six when Hagar gave birth to baby Ishmael.[4]

Thirteen years later, Abram had another encounter with God. God restated the promise that Abram, whose name means "father," would be the father of many peoples. God then gave him a new name, Abraham, which means "father of a multitude," and underscored this covenant relationship by calling Abraham to make a living offering of himself in the form of circumcision for himself and every male in his household. This intimate and dramatic act underscores the remarkable nature of the faith this ninety-nine-year-old man had with God. Abraham lived out this faith in this promise by making love to his eighty-nine-year-old wife, who, despite her own scorn and ongoing sorrow, was given a new identity as well. God changed her name from Sarai (princess), giving her a new, mature identity as Sarah, which means "noblewoman."

A new branch of the family tree budded when Isaac, the child of God's promise, was born to these two aging parents. In the ancient Near East, the oldest son carried both ruling authority within the clan and rights to the family estate. But God usurped cultural custom by underscoring that it was the younger of these two branches of Abraham's late-blooming family tree who would carry his father's promise to the next generation.

We see the pattern of a younger child elevated to the position of legal and spiritual authority over the elder repeated when the union of Isaac and his wife Rebecca[5] results in a set of fraternal twins they named Esau and Jacob. Like her mother-in-law Sarah, Rebecca dealt with infertility for many years, and when she finally became pregnant (and decidedly uncomfortable!) after Isaac's intercession, the Lord revealed to her that she would be having twins, and that the older one would serve the younger. The babies' names, Esau (which appears to mean "hairy") and Jacob (which means "supplanter" or "deceiver"), set their identities in motion. Scripture reports that macho Esau was favored by his father, and second-born Jacob by his mother. The promise Rebecca received while pregnant came to pass when the impulsive Esau made the decision to trade his legal birthright for a meal from his opportunistic younger brother Jacob (Genesis 25:27–34).

The family tree thus divided into two new branches, and Esau's descendants, the Edomites, became an ongoing generational annoyance to Jacob's family. Genesis 36 lists the domestic and legal genealogies of Esau's descendants, and notes that the tribe/nation that was part of Jacob's line moved east of Canaan, to land that is now part of modern-day Jordan.

As the carrier of God's promise to a new generation, Isaac gave Jacob the same direction his own father had given him: Do not marry an idol-worshiping local Canaanite woman, but instead find yourself a wife from among your mother's kin. After hearing the guidance his younger brother had received, Esau decided the only logical response, in order to demonstrate peak annoyance with the way things had gone in his family, was to do the opposite. He added a Canaanite descendant of Ishmael to his own group of wives (Genesis 28:1–9).

God's letters from home reveal very relatable human families with patterns of faithfulness and sin running like sap through the family tree. Jacob obeyed his father's counsel to seek a wife from among his mother's family and experienced a birth order reversal of his own when he sought to marry Rachel, the younger daughter of his uncle Laban, and discovered after the darkness of the wedding night that Laban had pulled a switcheroo and given him instead his older daughter Leah as a wife. Jacob became his bondslave in order to earn the privilege of marrying Rachel as well.

Married to the same man, the sister-wives became rivals as they each sought to bear Jacob's children. Each woman also put her own servant into the mix in an attempt to multiply offspring that would count as her own. Jacob's wives and their servants ultimately birthed twelve sons and one daughter to his line (Genesis 29:31–30:24).

Jacob had spent the first decades of his life in an adversarial relationship with his brother thanks to the obvious favoritism in which both their parents indulged, while simultaneously navigating his complex marriages. He'd grown accustomed to living by his wits, befitting his name as a supplanter or deceiver. But God had more in mind for him. Genesis 32:22–32 describes an all-night showdown this wily character had with God that brought Jacob to a place of full surrender. God changed his name from Jacob to Israel (which has been interpreted to mean "he strives with God" or "he prevails with God").

With the birth of Abraham's great-grandsons, the branch of Abraham's family tree that carried God's promise to Abraham burst into bloom. That complex cluster of branches carried the toxin of sibling rivalry, as ten of those brothers conspired to rid themselves of Jacob's eleventh son, Joseph. (Benjamin, the twelfth, was not involved in the plot.) The ten sold Joseph to a group of traders heading to Egypt. Jacob was led to believe his favorite son had been mauled to death, and ten of his sons held the truth in silence.

God sent them a letter postmarked "Egypt" when a regional famine drove the family from Canaan south to buy grain. They discovered that not only was Joseph still alive, but because of his willingness to listen to God's voice guiding him in his service to Egypt's king, he was responsible for the stockpiles of grain in the nation. He saved his family's lives.

Joseph's extended family sojourned in Egypt, and within a generation or two, all of Abraham's descendants were trapped in slavery, fulfilling the prophecy God had given to Abraham in Genesis 15:13. Despite the misery of their conditions, their numbers increased exponentially. Oral tradition carried their origins, relationships, and God's promise to each successive generation of slaves over the span of four centuries. The importance of family history is underscored throughout this first set of letters from home. Nine genealogies are listed in the book of Genesis (2:4; 5:1–32; 6:9; 10:1–32; 11:10–32; 25:12–13, 19–26; 36:1–43; 37:2).

Coming home, leaving home

Generations of Abraham's descendants were born into slavery, but there had always been an expiration date on their enslaved status. When it was time, a child from the tribe of Levi named Moses (Exodus 6:19–20) would be adopted and raised by one of Pharoah's daughters through the skillful maneuvering of Moses's mother Jochebed to save her infant son's life in the face of a genocidal death order. Jochebed then secured herself a position as Moses's wet nurse and as a result was able to teach him who he really was. That sense of identity carried him through the rest of his childhood, which he spent among Egyptian royalty (Exodus 2:1–10).

God would use Moses to lead Abraham's entire sprawling family out of Egypt, into the wilderness, and eventually toward freedom.[6] After four centuries of enslavement in Egypt, they spent forty years in the desert, where they learned to live in relationship with God through the Lord's presence and provision and by learning God's ways through the gift of the Law given at Mount Sinai.

The children of Israel relied on the domestic, legal, and religious genealogies they'd kept via oral tradition so they could organize themselves under God's rule when it came time to return to the Promised Land. The descendants of Levi, the third son of Jacob and Leah, were given the responsibility of serving as priests, leading the nation of siblings in prescribed worship to God (Exodus 28, Leviticus 8–10). While the land allotted to eleven of the tribes is described in Joshua 13–21, the Levites did not receive a portion of land, as God told them that he himself would be their inheritance (Deuteronomy 10:8–9).

As time went by, the people grew increasingly restless with God as their leader. All the other nations around them had kings to guide them. God warned the Israelites they would experience the consequences of choosing this path, but also noted that this path would pave the way for a leader like no human leader they'd ever known, who would function as prophet, priest, and king for the nation and save his people from their sin (1 Samuel 8:7–16; Psalm 89:3–4). The letter from home describing the lineage of Israel's kings told the people that every ruler would come from the line of Benjamin, the youngest of Jacob's children. The idea of a younger son in a position of authority was both countercultural in the ancient Near East and a theme familiar to the people of Israel, who knew it well from the account of the first three generations of Jacob's family tree.

Benjaminite Saul, son of Kish, was the first of Israel's kings, but after he disobeyed God's clear instructions, God's messenger Samuel told Saul that his line would come to an end and that God would raise up another king to rule over Israel (1 Samuel 15). That person was David, the youngest son of Jesse (1 Samuel 16:1–11). When David ascended to the throne after Saul and his sons were killed in battle, another prophet, Nathan, spoke a message to David that described the reign of one of his future descendants, which would be unlike that of any other king. God himself would be Father of this son, and his throne would endure forever (2 Samuel 7:11–16).

But that promise wouldn't be fulfilled immediately.[7] David's grandsons got involved in a power struggle after the death of their father Solomon, and the rivalry divided Israel into two kingdoms. The southern kingdom, known as Judah, contained Jerusalem and included the tribal lands of Judah and Benjamin. The northern kingdom continued to be known as Israel and contained the lands of the remaining tribes (1 Kings 12). This division among the extended family of Jacob set the stage for spiritual compromise that led to the invasion of Israel by the Assyrian army in 732 BC. The people of the north had long demonstrated their affection for the idol worship practiced by their neighbors. As a result, their love for the one true God had been extinguished. They lost their land and their identities as the Assyrians enslaved some and intermarried with others.

Judah was only slightly less spiritually compromised. Despite Jerusalem's function as the center of worship for the Hebrew people, too many in Judah coveted the gods of their idol-worshiping neighbors despite what had happened to their cousins living in the north. Prophetic voices warning Judah of a coming captivity also spoke of an unprecedented, supernatural return of the Hebrew people to their homeland (Jeremiah 25; 29:10). When the Babylonians invaded the weakened nation in a series of conquests from 597 to 586 BC, most of the people of Judah were marched into exile.

When it would have been easier for the captive people to assimilate, the experience of exile served to turn Judah back to wholehearted devotion to God.[8] After the people had spent seventy years in Babylon, King Cyrus announced that he would allow them to return to the land. This was a letter from home delivered through a foreign king.

The books of Ezra and Nehemiah record the details of this return. And it turns out, genealogical records played an integral part in this process. Ezra 2 offers a listing of the first wave of returnees and concludes with these words: "The priests, the Levites, the musicians, the gatekeepers and the temple servants settled in their own towns, along with some of the other people, and the rest of the Israelites settled in their towns" (v. 70). Though none of the returnees had ever lived in those towns, family history guided them as they resettled Judah.[9]

Living letter from home

For the next few centuries, the people of Judah were able to remain in the land. However, they lived almost entirely under the reign of foreign entities. When they did manage to regain control of their territory, political infighting and spiritual compromise again left them vulnerable to invasion and foreign control.[10] By 63 BC, Judah was living under oppressive Roman rule.

God sent Jesus, the ultimate letter from home, into that milieu. Genealogies were one essential way of certifying the authenticity and importance of that letter. The gospels of Matthew and Luke place genealogies front and center in order to establish Jesus' place in the family tree, situating him in the kingly line of David as well as connecting him to the prophetic descriptions of the Messiah ribboned throughout the Old Testament.

The genealogy of Jesus found in Matthew 1:1–17 begins with the first branch of the family tree of the Hebrew people, Abraham, tracing the lineage of Jesus through David and to Joseph, the husband of Mary, noting the rhyme of temporal time at the conclusion of the listing: "Thus there were fourteen generations in all from Abraham to David, fourteen from David to the exile to Babylon, and fourteen from the exile to the Messiah" (v. 17). Luke 3:23–38 works backward from Jesus to Adam, showing how Jesus, the Jewish Messiah, was born in the city of David not just for the descendants of Abraham, Isaac, and Jacob, but for all humankind.

The genealogy of Jesus found in the gospel of Matthew highlights the family story of Joseph, Jesus' legal father, establishing Jesus' Davidic heritage. One of the names in that lineage, Jeconiah, also known as Coniah, did not father any sons who ascended to the throne (1 Chronicles 3:16; Jeremiah 22:24–30; Matthew 1:12). Because of Jeconiah, Joseph's line alone would have disqualified Jesus from being in line for a kingly role. But Mary's genealogy, which Luke's account traces through her grandfather Eli (or Heli), establishing

Jesus' direct connection to David while bypassing the blunted dead end of Jeconiah, situates the fully human, fully divine Jesus in a different tributary of the royal Davidic line.[11]

The New Testament is sprinkled with references to the family story established through the twelve tribes of Israel. We see it in a promise Jesus made to his twelve disciples about sitting on twelve thrones alongside him, judging those twelve tribes (Matthew 19:28; Luke 22:30). It's there in Paul's defense before Rome's appointed Jewish leader Agrippa (Acts 26:7). The story appears in the apostle James's address to the dispersed readers of his epistle (James 1:1). And the final book of the New Testament highlights that family story in the description of the future New Jerusalem (Revelation 21:12).

Paul's letter to the Romans describes how Christ's life, death, and resurrection changed the very nature of his family tree. He explains to those outside the twelve tribes that they are now grafted into that family tree through Jesus (Romans 11). The epistles include a few cautions for those who focused on genealogies in divisive ways, reminding readers that because of the person and work of Jesus, those old debates about defining who was in and who was out of the family on the basis of bloodline were no longer relevant (Titus 3:9; 1 Timothy 1:4). As Paul prayed for the young church in Ephesus, he emphasized the relationship between each family and God: "For this reason I kneel before the Father, from whom every family in heaven and on earth derives its name" (Ephesians 3:14–15). It is faith in the risen Messiah, not bloodline, that forms this incredible family tree (Galatians 3:26–29).

Our final letter from home reveals what this family tree will look like in the end: "After this I looked, and there before me was a great multitude that no one could count, from every nation, tribe, people and language, standing before the throne and before the Lamb" (Revelation 7:9). Genesis 11 records the scattering, cacophony, and confusion that followed in the wake of the pride that went into building the Tower of Babel. After the resurrection of Jesus, the outpouring of the Holy Spirit, accompanied by the supernatural multilingual proclamation of the good news (Acts 2:1–13), was the beginning of the reversal of Babel's scattering. The final letter from home reminds us that in the presence of God, we will be one beloved, unified-but-diverse family, and our worship will need no translation.

Even among seasoned Bible readers, there is a tendency to see the sweep and scope of Scripture as something external to our own experience. After all, don't these letters from home exist to teach us about who God is?

That is one purpose, but it is not the only one. The Bible also exists to reveal who we are. The story of Scripture is our story as well. Every facet of our human condition is named and described within its pages. If God had meant those letters to be a one-way monologue, God would have guided the writers to report only his part of the story. But the Bible is not a shiny, tidy public relations press release. It reveals an unflinching look at the breadth of our shared humanity from the faith of Abram to the betrayal of Judas. It highlights the complexity of the interconnected relationships in our homes and communities. Even if we come from a long line of unbelievers, our family story is fully connected to God's story. God's letters from home are written to us, about us, and for us. They're foundational to our interpretative task. As we consider some of the primary threads that have been woven into our own family stories, we'll see the imprint of the Bible's themes entwined in those threads—all the way to the cellular level.

Reflect

1. What words would you use to describe the kinds of family stories found in Scripture? What do these kinds of stories tell you about the human family? About God?

2. What repeating patterns can you observe in the lives of the Old Testament patriarchs (Abraham, Isaac, and Jacob)? Why might this be significant as you consider your own family story?

3. How would you explain to a young child how Jesus' life, death, and resurrection changed how families from every tongue, tribe, and nation could relate to God? How might that understanding be of help as you seek to translate your family story?

THREE

~

Decoding the Double Helix

Deciphering the Language of Our DNA

DURING THE PAST CENTURY and a half, humankind has begun to learn to speak the language of our DNA. We've come a long way from the observations of monk Gregor Mendel drawn from his selective breeding of pea plants in the mid-1800s that became foundational to the study of genetics. Just 150 years later, the Human Genome Project mapped the entire human genome, sequencing the 3.2 billion combinations of the four basic chemical building blocks of DNA: adenine (A); cytosine (C), guanine (G), and thymine (T). Nowadays it might be hard to remember a time when doctors, scientists, law enforcement, and the general public weren't learning to listen to and begin to translate what A, C, G, and T have been telling us all along.

Today, the translator's task might begin at the cellular level. More than thirty million people worldwide have taken consumer DNA tests over the past couple of decades.[1] The results of these tests highlight our ethnic ancestry and suggest possible DNA connections with others who've taken the same test.[2] Consumer and medical genetic testing have illuminated parts of our family stories that were once hidden in the shadows of rumor or obscured by silence.

Science writer Sam Kean suggests that our genes are the story, and our DNA is the language in which the story is written.[3] I'd amend his words just a bit to say that our genes tell an important part of the story, and DNA is a primary but not solitary language in which our story is written. Even so, Kean notes, "Every human activity leaves a trace in our DNA, and whether that DNA records stories about music or sports or Machiavellian microbes, those tales tell, collectively, a larger and more intricate tale of the rise of human beings on Earth: why we're one of nature's most absurd creatures, as well as its crowning glory."[4]

We inherit all kinds of physical characteristics from our forebears: a gap-toothed smile, blue eyes, jet-black hair. But throughout our entire lifetime, A, C, G, and T are continuing their conversation in our bodies. As researchers learn to listen to what they're telling us, we are beginning to unlock relevant information they hold about everything from our health to our heritage.

For example, I spent quite a bit of my childhood and at least half of every year of my adult life on antibiotics for what seemed at the time an unending series of upper respiratory and sinus infections, with a few cases of life-threatening pneumonia thrown in for good measure. When I was in my mid-fifties, a pulmonologist ordered a blood test that revealed that my body was missing some key components of my immune system and diagnosed me with a rare immune system disorder. Eventually, another doctor involved in research ordered a genetic test that would examine 207 genes connected with some known immunodeficiencies. The test revealed that I did indeed have a genetic variant that has played havoc with my immune system, though the test couldn't determine whether it was hereditary or whether it was a spontaneous mutation. The results of that genetic test probably won't change things during my lifetime, but the information will contribute to the ongoing study of DNA that is shedding new light on all kinds of inherited conditions.[5]

Many, many other disorders have their origins in our DNA, ranging from rare health conditions like hemophilia, a blood clotting disorder, to far more common expressions of genetic heritability such as certain breast cancers. My long-time friends, identical twins Charm Britton and Teri Graszer, have been the subjects of ongoing genetic studies because there have been five generations of breast or ovarian cancer in their family, including Charm's breast cancer diagnosis just two weeks before their mother died of ovarian cancer. The ages at which the women in their family have been diagnosed continues to trend younger. Teri's daughter Pam died of Stage 4 breast cancer before she was thirty. Though the family tested negative for the BRCA1 and BRCA2 genes that researchers have linked to the disease, doctors believe there is a genetic link to the prevalence of breast cancer in the family. They just haven't discovered what it is yet.

Other conditions such as Down syndrome and osteogenesis imperfecta (brittle bone disease) are transmitted via DNA.

Because of the long history of intermarriage within the Jewish community, there is a far-higher-than-average concentration of some rare genetic disorders, such as Tay-Sachs disease, a condition that is typically fatal by a child's fifth birthday.[6] As part of their premarital preparation, many Jewish couples undergo genetic testing in order to screen for the disease.

Scientists have also discovered what appears to be a genetically transmitted predisposition toward addiction and some forms of mental illness, although nurture, environment, and intervention can change that script. At a wedding a few years ago, I offered a glass of wine to a guest so he could join in toasting the newlyweds. He waved it off, noting without malice, "I choose not to drink, because my parents and grandparents were all addicts, and I strongly suspect I wouldn't be able to stop if I ever started." His awareness of his family history led him to take preemptive action.

Just as a doctor will take a cursory family medical history on an intake visit with a new patient, so our own personal assessment of our family's genetic history should include generational patterns of physical disease, mental health struggle, and addiction. As we do this, it is helpful to keep in mind the scene from near the end of Charles Dickens's beloved book *A Christmas Carol*, when the Ghost of Christmas Future shows the miserable, stingy Ebenezer Scrooge a vision of Scrooge's neglected grave. Scrooge asks the ghost, "Why show me this, if I am past all hope?"

In that moment, Scrooge recognizes that his past does not have to be his future. This is one area of our lives where we need advanced translation skills. It is one thing to decode what A, C, G, and T might be saying to and about us. It is another level entirely to discern what can and can't be changed regarding the DNA we inherit so we can live well in light of that information.

Secrets revealed

Because of the rapid advance of genetic studies, DNA is no longer a vault of inaccessible secrets the way it was even a couple of generations ago.

Philip Anderson[7] planned to take his secret to the grave with him. But seven decades after he fathered a child when he was sixteen, the results of a commercial DNA test revealed the truth.

The child's name was Kathleen.

"Kathleen's daughter Maria reached out to me via Facebook," said Tracy, Philip's daughter with his wife of more than sixty years—and Kathleen's younger half-sister. "My father never told my mother that he knew he got a girl pregnant in his teens. In fact, he'd never told anyone, including his own parents. My dad never knew what happened to the girl, because she moved away, then wrote to him to tell him that she was pregnant. He remembers writing back to her once but didn't offer her any help. He put the whole thing out of his mind and got on with his life."

Kathleen was placed for adoption by her teen mother and grew up in a loving family. But like many adoptees, Kathleen always wondered about her birth parents and had been searching for them for years. Her commercial DNA test and some detective work by her daughter Maria led her to the name of her birth mother, but the pair learned that she had died several years earlier. Their search also led them to a cousin of Kathleen's birth father and, eventually, to Tracy's Facebook page. "She was concerned that reaching out to my father at his advanced age might be too much of a shock, so she contacted me first."

Tracy asked her father if what Maria and Kathleen shared could be true. "I didn't know if my mother was aware of this, so I asked him privately," she said. It turned out that her mother didn't know anything about this chapter of her husband's life. "There is so much sadness in the story, and it has been challenging for all of us to process it," Tracy said.

I know from my own experience regarding the secrecy around my mom's adoption that processing the truth of a reconfigured past is an ongoing task for everyone in a family. Tracy noted that her younger brother still struggles with a sense of betrayal and remains uncomfortable with the cordial relationship their parents and Tracy have developed with Kathleen and her family. Both Tracy and her mother report that their initial shock faded and a sense of compassion grew as they acknowledged the social pressures at play during the era when Kathleen was conceived.

One significant hurdle to the budding relationship between Philip and Kathleen occurred shortly after they first connected. "My half-sister was under the impression that my father was never told about the pregnancy because of some information on the adoption papers she received as she did her research," Tracy said. "We learned this before my father actually talked with Kathleen, so he did not tell her at first that he actually was informed of the pregnancy when he was sixteen. He thought that it might be hurtful for her to learn that he did know but did nothing to help." Tracy and her mom urged Phillip to tell his newfound daughter the truth—that he had known that Kathleen's mother was pregnant with her. Tracy noted that Kathleen was philosophical about the social pressures faced by both her teen birth parents: "She recognizes that my dad was an insecure and very scared teenager." Consumer DNA tests have brought all kinds of stories like Phillip and Kathleen's to the fore. In an op-ed on the subject for the *Washington Post*, writer Libby Copeland observes, "Here's the thing about those unexpected discoveries: The reality of our genes may collide with the narratives we hold dear. We construct stories about who we are and what we value; about our parents' characters and our spouses' loyalties. The results of consumer genetic testing can serve as Rorschach tests for our beliefs about family, morality and the past."[8]

A commercial DNA test revealed that the man who raised memoirist Dani Shapiro was not her biological father. Her 2019 memoir, *Inheritance: A Memoir of Genealogy, Paternity, and Love*, follows Shapiro as she pieces together the clues not only from her Ancestry results but also from snatches of conversations with family members and her own skilled internet sleuthing. She discovered that in 1961–62, her parents sought help to conceive a child from a fertility clinic. The practice of artificial insemination was in its infancy, and the clinic that Shapiro's parents chose had a practice of mixing the sperm of anonymous medical school donors with that of the father. Shapiro discovered that her biological father was one of those medical students. Shapiro, reflecting on the dynamics in her family during her childhood, writes, "All my life I had known there was a secret. What I hadn't known: the secret was me."[9]

If you watch true crime television shows, you'll learn that DNA can be used today to crack even decades-old cold cases. And sometimes, genetic evidence can prove or disprove rumors that have persisted for more than two hundred years.

American history school texts cite the accomplishments of founding father Thomas Jefferson: he was one of the drafters of the Declaration of Independence, he was the country's third president, and he negotiated with France the Louisiana Purchase, which at the time of its signing doubled the territory belonging to the United States. In the pages of most of those books, he is celebrated as a man ahead of his time.

But in other ways, he was a man *of* his time and place. For one, we know that he claimed as property approximately 175 human beings who worked his plantation at Monticello, near Charlottesville, Virginia.

Rumors about his relationship with one of those enslaved women circulated as early as 1801, shortly after he was sworn into office. James Callender wrote in the *Richmond Recorder* in September 1, 1801: "And in regards to his slave, Sally Hemmings. As early as IT is well known that the man, *whom it delighteth the people to honor,* keeps, and for many years past has kept, as his concubine, one of his own slaves. Her name is SALLY."[10]

Rumors about the relationship between Jefferson and Hemings persisted for generations. In 1998, a team of researchers did genetic testing among several known descendants of Hemings and of Jefferson and found there was a high probability that Jefferson was indeed the father of Hemings's children.[11]

More than two centuries after the time of Hemings and Jefferson, Britni Danielle wrote a *Washington Post* piece challenging the attempt by some historians to frame the sexual relationship between enslaver and enslaved as consensual: "Language like that elides the true nature of their relationship, which is believed to have begun when Hemings, then

14 years old, accompanied Jefferson's daughter to live with Jefferson, then 44, in Paris. She wasn't Jefferson's mistress; she was his property. And he raped her."[12]

Other scholars have challenged this narrative by pointing to the fact that Hemings appears to have chosen to leave Paris, where she enjoyed the legal status of a free person, to return to Virginia and enslavement at Monticello. Historians believe that after the death of Jefferson's wife in 1782, Jefferson fathered at least six children with Hemings. Four survived to adulthood. Of all the people whom Jefferson enslaved, only Hemings and her children were granted freedom or allowed to leave without pursuit near the end of Jefferson's life or shortly after his death.[13]

The descendants of Sally Hemings are far from the only African Americans carrying the DNA of a white European enslaver. Michael White, assistant professor of genetics at Washington University School of Medicine in St. Louis, writes, "Widespread sexual exploitation of slaves before the Civil War strongly influenced the genetic make-up of essentially all African Americans alive today."[14] On average, African Americans have 24 percent European ancestry, traced most often through the line of a male.[15] Results of DNA testing shine an unblinking spotlight on the actions of enslavers who believed they had rights to every square inch of the women's bodies in their possession. Those results also speak powerfully about the strength and determination of the mothers who birthed and nurtured their children in the cruel and immoral conditions created by those who enslaved other human beings.

As the science of fertility has developed, there have been other shocking, unexpected consequences. Some serial sperm donors have fathered as many as two hundred children. Consumer DNA tests and social media have helped some curious biological half-siblings connect with one another. A 2019 *New York Times Magazine* piece profiles one such group of thirty-two half-siblings conceived by the sperm of a single donor. The photos accompanying the article, taken by one of those offspring, Eli Baden-Lazar, are fascinating in both the physical similarities and the differences they display. Baden-Lazar, who met with and captured images of his half-siblings, writes, "Looking through the camera, I had a feeling I couldn't shake: that these people were all versions of me, just formed in different parts of the country—but were also strangers who might as well have been picked out of a hat."[16]

The letters A, C, G, and T murmur and sometimes shout stories about our origins that may be entirely predictable thanks to family lore or may contain secrets or surprises, like dozens of biological half-siblings. Those letters in our flawed and beautiful world may carry the code for disease or disability. But grounding the discussion is the reality that each human being bears the *imago Dei*, the image of God. As professor of government and philosopher J. Budziszewski writes, "Trying to understand man without recognizing him as the *imago Dei* is like trying to understand a bas-relief without recognizing it as a carving."[17]

Taking a jackhammer to a bas-relief

As our understanding about genetics has grown during the past 150 years, some dark applications of the science have emerged. Those applications have been the equivalent of taking a jackhammer to that metaphorical bas-relief, not only ignoring the reality that the sculpture is a carving created by a Master Artist but also obliterating its beauty in an attempt to engineer an entirely new kind of human. Gregor Mendel's mid-nineteenth-century discoveries about how peas could be bred selectively in order to develop plants that yielded specific traits have led to other remarkable scientific discoveries, including the discovery and diagnosis of viruses, targeted gene therapy for diseases like cancer, and advances in forensic science to crack decades-old cold cases.[18] Mendel's very good discoveries were also applied to a very, very bad idea.

That idea is eugenics.

The word was coined from the Greek words for "good" and "birth." Eugenics is the practice of applying the principles of selective breeding to the human race in order to eradicate "weak links" from the gene pool and reproduce only what is deemed desirable. The word *eugenics* was first coined by a cousin of Charles Darwin named Francis Galton. In his 1869 book *Hereditary Genius: An Inquiry into Its Laws and Consequences*, Galton said that better breeding would give the world a better race of human beings, noting that as it was "easy . . . to obtain by careful selection a permanent breed of dogs or horses gifted with peculiar powers of running, or of doing anything else, so it would be quite practicable to produce a highly-gifted race of men by judicious marriages during several consecutive generations."[19]

Galton's idea found a ready home among the intelligentsia of the early twentieth century. In the United States, Cold Spring Harbor, New York, became the home of three eugenics-themed centers of study: the Biological Laboratory, the Station for Experimental Evolution, and the Eugenics Records Office. The latter was involved during the first decades of the 1900s in advocating for mandatory sterilizations of those deemed undesirable and exhorting the government to restrict immigration.[20]

British writer G. K. Chesterton sounded the moral alarm around the issue of eugenics in 1922: "When I speak of Eugenic legislation, or the coming of the Eugenic State, they think of it as something like *The Time Machine* or *Looking Backward*: a thing that, good or bad, will have to fit itself to their great-great-great-grandchild, who may be very different and may like it; and who in any case is rather a distant relative. To all this I have, to begin with, a very short and simple answer. The Eugenic State has begun."[21] He was correct to be alarmed, but he was wrong about the speed by which these ideas would take root in Western culture. It wouldn't take generations for these ideas to take hold.

In 1927, the Supreme Court determined that individual state governments could require women whom the state deemed unfit to be forcibly sterilized. The policies and practices that emerged from this decision resulted in nearly three-quarters of U.S. states enforcing sterilization laws that were either pending or on the books by 1935.[22] All told, as many as seventy thousand Americans were forcibly sterilized during the twentieth century. These victims included those branded as "imbeciles" or "promiscuous" as well as those who were blind, deaf, and diseased. Authorities disproportionately targeted minorities and the poor.[23]

The last forced sterilization in the United States occurred in 1981.[24] There have been efforts in states like California, which was a center of eugenics research, to legislate some form of financial reparations to the survivors or family of those who underwent forced sterilizations, but passage of these bills has moved at a snail's pace.[25]

Adolph Hitler credited the eugenics movement in the United States for the "scientific" support of his own racial policies. In 1931, Nazi elite guard, known as the SS, created the Race and Settlement Office in order to find "racially acceptable" so-called Aryan (Germanic or Nordic) spouses for SS officers.[26] In 1933, Hitler's new government passed the Law for the Prevention of Genetically Diseased Offspring, which led to the forced sterilizations of four hundred thousand German citizens. In 1935, the Nuremberg Laws (one of which was coined the "Blood Protection Law"), criminalized marriage between Gentile Germans and groups deemed to be racially inferior, which included the Roma as well as Jewish people.[27] By 1945, six million Jews and another six million "undesirables" had perished in the Holocaust. Eugenics was foundational to the Nazi philosophy.

A very, very bad idea has had history-altering consequences that echo to this day. There are too many family trees with limbs that have been severed violently and abruptly.

We carry the *imago Dei* in our DNA

When I gave birth to my first child, I cradled her in my arms and looked for signs of family resemblance. Did she inherit my curly hair? My husband's blue eyes? How had God combined our respective DNA to create a brand-new human being?

Eugene Peterson's *The Message* paraphrase of Psalm 139:13–16 captures the awestruck response our creator God deserves as we welcome each new life to this world:

Oh yes, you shaped me first inside, then out;
you formed me in my mother's womb.

I thank you, High God—you're breathtaking!
　Body and soul, I am marvelously made!
　I worship in adoration—what a creation!
You know me inside and out,
　you know every bone in my body;
You know exactly how I was made, bit by bit,
　how I was sculpted from nothing into something.
Like an open book, you watched me grow from
　conception to birth;
　all the stages of my life were spread out before you,
The days of my life all prepared
　before I'd even lived one day.

Perhaps even more remarkable is that no two of us are exactly alike. Dr. Francis Collins, who was the head of the Human Genome Project and, more recently, the director of the National Institutes of Health, notes that humankind is 99.9 percent identical at the DNA level, which makes our incredible diversity even more breathtaking. DNA tells the story of biological inheritance, but it is written in the language of the Creator, according to Collins. The genome, he writes, is "a book of instructions, a record of history, a medical textbook. . . . This book was written in the DNA language by which God spoke life into being. I felt an overwhelming sense of awe in surveying this most significant of all biological texts. Yes, it is written in a language we understand very poorly, and it will take decades, if not centuries, to understand its instructions."[28]

We may not currently comprehend much of what this language is saying to us, but the breathtaking beauty of its complexity, precision, and power as an expression of creation is an essential way we can attune ourselves to the One whose Word birthed the world and everything in it (Genesis 1–2; John 1:1–5). Every living thing on the planet bears the DNA imprint of its Creator, and humankind carries the additional blessing and responsibility of being created in God's image.

This truth doesn't excuse in any way those who have frittered away their God-gifted dignity by doing cruel, sinful things, past or present. Nor is that truth eroded by genetic mutations, illness or disease, or assistance from modern reproductive technology. Our family's image-bearing story is not diminished by its genetic history but rather is a reflection of our human condition. While there is brokenness in every human's history, there is also goodness that reflects the imprint of our Maker.

Translating the past must be grounded in the understanding that we as well as our forebears carry intrinsic worth and dignity because each one of us carries the language of *imago Dei* in our DNA.

Reflect

1. Have you or anyone in your family taken a consumer or medical DNA test? If you have, did the results surprise you? Understanding that the science behind DNA is still in its infancy, what kinds of results would you like to see from future genetic tests?

2. As you consider the subject of eugenics, what questions do you have about the topic? Why do you believe the ideas found such a broad audience during the twentieth century?

3. Below you'll find a listing of some key scripture passages that speak to the topic of the *imago Dei*. What does each tell you about God? About humankind? About your own family story?

- Genesis 1:26–28
- Job 33
- John 1:1–5, 18
- Romans 1:20–23
- Romans 8:29
- 2 Corinthians 3:18
- Colossians 1:15
- *For further study:* 1 Corinthians 15

FOUR

The Unwanted "Gift" That Keeps Giving

Understanding How Trauma Can Encode Itself into Our Family History

E ITHER YOU'RE GOING to call Child Protective Services or I will."

The counselor let her words hang in the air. Ingrid[1] had confessed that she'd been physically and verbally abusive toward one of her young children. The encounter had put the child in danger.

It wasn't the first time.

But this time, Ingrid, overwhelmed by the realization that her desire to give her children a happy childhood was short-circuiting in ways she couldn't have imagined and couldn't seem to control, had reached out to a counselor for help. Ingrid's counselor explained that she had a legal responsibility to report to Child Protective Services or the police if a child was in danger—and she felt that Ingrid's children were not safe with her. She told Ingrid she thought it would go better for Ingrid with the state if Ingrid herself chose to make the call.

That call was a turning point in Ingrid's life as she began to recognize that she needed help to recognize, grieve, and integrate the trauma of her childhood so she could rescript the patterns that seemed to be hardwired into her life.

Pulling together the threads of our family stories includes learning to listen to the language of trauma in our own lives as well as the lives of our forebears. That language has many different dialects and accents, and it requires empathy to begin to decode it.

In Ingrid's case, the trauma began generations before she was conceived. Ingrid was born to a nineteen-year-old teenage runaway who had fled her childhood home in order to escape an abusive, alcoholic father. Ingrid's father was a thirty-five-year-old man who liked to date much younger women. Her parents never married, splitting up shortly after Ingrid was born. They shared custody of their daughter, but that arrangement changed when Ingrid was two and a half. Ingrid's father was on the phone with Ingrid's mother when he heard her slap their toddler daughter across the face.

After that incident, Ingrid's father became her primary caregiver and brought her to the home he shared with his mother. Then, shortly before Ingrid's third birthday, her mother died in a car accident. There were hints that it might have been a suicide attempt. Officials at the scene found a box of cake mix and a birthday candle in the shape of the number three on the front seat of the car.

Ingrid's paternal grandmother was a stabilizing influence in her life but didn't appear to know that her son—Ingrid's father—was sexually abusing Ingrid throughout her childhood. In addition, Ingrid's father had gotten into a new relationship with another young adult woman, who sometimes served as Ingrid's part-time nanny. This girlfriend/nanny drifted in and out of the home for several years. Then, when Ingrid was seven, her grandmother's house caught fire. The family was able to move back in several months later, but it was yet another destabilizing event in the little girl's tumultuous life.

As Ingrid headed into her middle school years, her grandmother's health began to fail. Ingrid worried that she'd lose the one person who provided her a measure of constancy and care. When Ingrid was thirteen, and in the midst of her grandmother's health crisis, Ingrid's father died of a sudden heart attack. After that, Ingrid spent the next two years taking care of her grandmother, who died when Ingrid was fifteen. Some neighbors took in the orphaned young woman so she would have a place to live while she finished high school. Ingrid managed to do so and was accepted into college.

During her sophomore year, a friend invited Ingrid to her church. Ingrid was captivated by the gospel message and confessed her faith in Christ. Within months, she put her studies on hold so she could travel with a group that visited college campuses proclaiming a strong anti-abortion message. The radical nature of the group appealed to her, and the family-like ethos in the organization salved some of the open, oozing wounds she was just beginning to recognize she carried.

In the years that followed, her new faith gave her the courage to marry and start a family. She longed to give her kids a childhood different from the one she had. But she realized that this desire alone wasn't enough to staunch the wounds she incurred during her childhood. The counseling she received in adulthood addressed that, and also helped her identify that her parents' poor choices were also a result of trauma in their respective pasts—trauma that had been passed from generation to generation via both experiences and genetics. Ingrid has spent nearly two decades since she made that phone call to Child Protective Services at the behest of her counselor doing the hard and healing work of translating the past to write a new story for herself, her children, and the generations yet to come.

The "gift" that keeps giving

Trauma can enter our lives through a single event, such as a car accident or sexual assault, or it can be a series of events, like the aftermath of a natural disaster, or an ongoing environment of crisis or abuse, like Ingrid experienced. In the wake of a traumatic event, shock can temporarily buffer the horror, and denial can slow the speed at which we absorb and process it. The American Psychological Association notes that longer-term responses to trauma can include unstable, erratic emotions, vivid flashbacks, and physical issues like headaches, sleep disturbances, and nausea.[2] Trauma can be like a set of Russian nesting dolls, or *matryoshka*. It can present itself again and again in our lives, distorting the message in our family story.

Trauma expert Dr. Bessel van der Kolk notes that many of us carry significant trauma: "One does not have to be a combat soldier or visit a refugee camp in Syria or the Congo to encounter trauma. Trauma happens to us, our friends, our families, and our neighbors. Research by the Centers for

Disease Control and Prevention has shown that one in five Americans was sexually molested as a child; one in four was beaten by a parent to the point of a mark being left on their body; and one in three couples engages in physical violence. A quarter of us grew up with alcoholic relatives, and one out of eight witnessed their mother being beaten or hit."[3]

Post-traumatic stress disorder (PTSD) can manifest itself in a person's body and mind in a variety of ways, including replaying the trauma as if it were happening in the present moment, attempting to bury the painful ordeal and behave as though it never happened, and countless variations between those two ends of the spectrum. A person with PTSD may have flattened emotions or be prone to intense negative emotions and actions. Some people with PTSD may also be dealing simultaneously with other issues, such as addiction or other mental illness diagnoses.

The diagnosis of complex PTSD, or c-PTSD, is reserved for those who've experienced traumatic circumstances, typically during childhood, over a long period, as Ingrid did. As with other forms of PTSD, many with that diagnosis are also dealing with other mental health issues. Complex PTSD can manifest in a variety of often self-destructive behaviors, including impulse control, acting out sexually, eating disorders, and addiction, as well as emotional challenges such as rage or depression, and mental struggles that can include amnesia and dissociation.[4]

Van der Kolk notes, "For many people the war begins at home: Each year about three million children in the United States are reported as victims of child abuse and neglect. One million of these cases are serious and credible enough to force local child protective services or the courts to take action.

In other words, for every soldier who serves in a war zone abroad, there are ten children who are endangered in their own homes. This is particularly tragic, since it is very difficult for growing children to recover when the source of terror and pain is not enemy combatants but their own caretakers."[5]

Trauma doesn't reside solely in stories as intense as Ingrid's. The COVID-19 pandemic has been a traumatic experience for the entire world. Other events, such as school shootings, leave trauma in their wake for those directly affected as well as some of those whose lives are interlaced with theirs. Things like unexpected job loss, divorce, abandonment, or relocation can leave their mark on a person's life and change the arc of a family's story.

Some families retell their histories in ways that don't account for the trauma experienced by their ancestors. For example, trauma lurks within the mythic story of a brave Irish great-great-grandfather who boarded a boat at the height of the potato famine and came to America with two dollars in his pocket, eventually making his way west to help build the railroads crisscrossing the country. The family may rightly celebrate Great-Great-Grandfather Patrick McKenna's pluck and courage, but a closer examination of his story can reveal the losses Patrick experienced.[6]

The Irish potato famine claimed the lives of more than a million people, including some in Patrick's family and village. Patrick had to leave hearth and home, knowing he'd probably never see his people again. The steerage-class voyage was rough, and one of his fellow passengers died on the journey. When Patrick disembarked in New York, he was robbed on his second day in the city. The young man experienced discrimination and bullying, as Patrick and the others in the wave of Irish immigrants were viewed with hostility by some other Americans. He was homesick, and he often found solace in the bottle. When he married and settled down in Topeka, Kansas, his wife and four children lived with a man who worked too hard and drank too much. He died in an accident at work when he was just forty-eight years old.

Patrick's immigrant hero story may endure within his family, but so does his unprocessed trauma. His daughter married an alcoholic. One of his sons ended up in prison. His other two sons, drawing on their father's pattern of hard work and determination, were able to build a better life than their father had.

"When those in our family have experienced unbearable traumas or have suffered with immense guilt or grief, the feelings can be overwhelming and can escalate beyond what they can manage or resolve," says counselor Mark Wolynn. "It's human nature: when pain is too great, people tend to avoid it. Sometimes, pain submerges until it can find a pathway for expression or resolution."[7] According to Wolynn, that pain may present itself in subsequent generations. He notes that in addition to trauma being passed from generation to generation, patterns of engaging or avoiding trauma's pain can also be passed down. One generation's unprocessed grief may become the next generation's unexplainable tendency toward anger.

Wolynn adds, "It helps to know what happened in our family that made our parents hurt so much. What sat behind the distance, criticism, or aggression in the first place? Knowing these events can open the door to understanding their pain, as well as our own. When we know the traumatic events that contributed to our parents' pain, our understanding and compassion can begin to overshadow the old hurts."[8]

Hitching a ride on our DNA

For generations, various academic disciplines ranging from the hard sciences to philosophy have debated whether human beings are shaped more by nature or by nurture. Those on Team Nature cite hereditary factors as the primary determiners of a person's identity and experience. In contrast, those belonging to Team Nurture recognize the ways that human beings are shaped most powerfully by social, environmental, and cultural factors. Though each team acknowledges the strength and power of the other team's players, the contest has continued as each team makes its case for dominance.

A newer field of scientific inquiry called epigenetics has blurred the lines between Team Nature and Team Nurture. The National Human Genome Research Institute defines epigenetics as a study of "heritable changes caused by the activation and deactivation of genes without any change in the underlying DNA sequence of the organism. The word *epigenetics* is of Greek origin and literally means over and above (epi) the genome."[9]

Research scientist David Allis noted in an interview, "There's an epigenetic code, just like there's a genetic code. There are codes to make parts of the genome more active, and codes to make them inactive."[10] Every living organism turns on and off its own specific genes throughout its life span. Researchers have discovered that information hitchhikes atop our DNA, passing from one generation to the next. This information holds a record of, among other things, trauma, shock, and loss.

The inherited epigenetic data we carry has been linked with various disease processes, including cancer, cardiovascular disease, autoimmune disorders, and reproductive issues. Lifestyle choices, including diet and sleep, can cause epigenetic changes, as can environmental factors, such as exposure to heavy metals, pesticides, tobacco smoke, bacteria, and viruses.[11] Experiences of trauma can cause epigenetic change as well. Trauma itself isn't being replicated, but a measurable and heightened sensitivity to certain triggers can be passed on to future generations. An early study documented what is believed to be epigenetic change in the children and grandchildren of those who'd survived the combination of war and severe famine in the Netherlands. No one was surprised that the severely malnourished children who'd survived the *Hongerwinter* (hunger winter) during World War II experienced chronic health issues after the war. The children born to women who'd lived through the Hongerwinter also presented significantly higher than expected rates of health problems, including obesity, diabetes, and mental illness. But scientists were surprised to discover that the grandchildren of Hongerwinter survivors also had significantly higher rates of health issues, even though the famine and war had happened two generations earlier. "Genes cannot change in an entire population in just two generations," Allis said. "But some memory of metabolic stress could have become heritable."[12]

Studies have found that environmental factors such as income and diet alone do not fully account for the higher level of infant mortality in the Black community in the United States. Scientists are discovering the connection between the constant vigilance Black people have reported as they've navigated life in American culture and adverse health outcomes in the next generation.[13] The long and difficult history of racism in this country begets trauma that is carried to new generations. That trauma reveals itself in a pattern of lower birth weights and higher levels of cortisol, the stress hormone, present in the systems of a disproportionate number of Black newborns.[14]

Not every physical and psychological effect found in children and grandchildren of those who survived a trauma like war can be tied to epigenetic changes, but emerging research is corroborating the wide-ranging ways in which the effects of these events can carry from one generation to the next. Grief, fear, and privation leave indelible marks in the stories of many families—whether the family talks about those experiences or chooses silence in the name of "moving on" and attempting to rebuild their lives. Both patterns of behavior and biochemical reactions leave their imprint in subsequent generations.

I've known children and grandchildren of Holocaust survivors, and a significant percentage has reported that their family members made the decision not to talk about what had happened to them, either to try to protect their children from the horror or to attempt to avoid reliving the memories, or both. Writer Myra Goodman describes the cost she has paid for her survivor parents' choice not to speak of their experiences: "The silence my parents kept did not protect me from inheriting a legacy of trauma. I've lived most of my life in a state of constant low-grade terror—always fearful, anxiously awaiting the next massive catastrophe. Only recently have I learned that my fear is a trauma symptom, and that in addition to trauma being passed down through behavioral patterns, catastrophic events alter the body's chemistry, and that these changes can be epigenetically transmitted to future generations."[15]

Jewish, Black, and Indigenous Americans have each been the focus of recent studies in epigenetics. All are populations that have experienced generations of ongoing trauma. But each one of us carries a measure of trauma within us. Writer Sherri Mitchell, a member of the Penawahpskek (Penobscot) Nation, offers some wise perspective about this reality. She writes, "When we don't allow ourselves to acknowledge the pain—the deep, agonizing soul pain that results from historical trauma— we aren't able to recognize that we are all carrying some measure of that pain within us. Instead, we allow it to isolate us and keep us cut off from one another. We also fail to recognize that the cause of that pain is not only a violation against us, it is a violation against life itself, and its mournful cries echo through our DNA, and become lodged in our genetic memory."[16]

Although at first glance it may seem as though epigenetic trauma steals potential from our lives because of the experiences of our forebears, researchers are discovering that just as epigenetic trauma is caused by an organism's negative interaction with its environment, so can positive intervention change the biological script for subsequent generations.[17]

Since the day Ingrid made that phone call to Child Protective Services at the behest of her counselor, her adulthood has been a study in how intervention can begin to rewrite a family story. Repeating patterns of addiction, abuse, and upheaval existed in earlier generations on both sides of her family. Ongoing, intensive individual and family counseling, nutritional support, accountability with a circle of caring friends, a deepening faith, and a steady marriage have given her children a very different life from what Ingrid had. Ingrid has continued to learn how to translate her trauma into the unfamiliar new language of wholeness.

Mark Wolynn notes that the genesis of every human being is biologically present two generations before we are born:

> In your earliest biological form, as an unfertilized egg, you already share a cellular environment with your mother and grandmother. When your grandmother was five months pregnant with your mother, the precursor cell of the egg you developed from was already present in your mother's ovaries.
>
> This means that before your mother was even born, your mother, your grandmother, and the earliest traces of you were all in the same body—three generations sharing the same biological environment. . . . Your inception can be similarly traced in your paternal line. The precursor cells of the sperm you developed from were present in your father when he was a fetus in his mother's womb.[18]

In addition, imagine this: Researchers have found that a child's genetic material remains in the mother's body for years after the baby is delivered. This is true even in the case of miscarriages.[19]

Past, present, and future are communicating between generations in ways we can scarcely comprehend.

Why, Lord?

There is no handy custom-made Rosetta Stone that will decrypt the different kinds of trauma written in our specific family stories. The historical Rosetta Stone is a basalt tablet discovered in 1799 that gave archaeologists and researchers the key to the code of what had been to that point undecipherable Egyptian hieroglyphics. This stone was created in the second century BC and contains a repeated message from Macedonian king Ptolemy V Epiphanes, who was ruling Egypt at the time. The message on this stone is in three languages: Greek, Demotic, which was a known Egyptian language, and the mysterious pictorial images of hieroglyphics. When the Rosetta Stone was discovered in 1799, seeing the three languages side by side gave researchers the ability to crack the code of the hieroglyphs.[20]

The interpretative tools we have at our disposal as we reflect on our family stories do not come with a personalized Rosetta Stone. There are no easy answers. But our questions can orient our interpretation of the events we're considering.

As I've acknowledged the places where pain has marked my family's narrative, I've had to navigate larger questions about why a good God has permitted bad things to happen to my forebears, to me, or to any of us. Those questions are much broader in nature than this book can cover and deserve a further examination. Appendix B suggests some resources for those who want to engage them more deeply.

Sometimes, well-meaning Jesus-following people shy away from voicing unanswerable questions because they believe those questions exhibit a lack of faith. But the Bible is full of questions, whether it is the lament found in the Psalms or the poetic exchanges of the book of Job.

I've found Job's story an especially helpful way to orient myself to asking questions. Just as the suffering that came into Job's life was never fully explained to him, so there are some things for which we will never have answers in our lives. The book of the Bible containing his story gives readers an interpretive key in the first chapter when we learn that Satan has been permitted to test God's faithful friend Job.

This man loses family, property, health, and reputation and never finds out why. Others seek to give him their answers to that question, but Job knows their answers are meant primarily to shame him. And their answers were wrong.

When God speaks into the confusion, Job is reminded that God's ways are not like Job's. Can Job trust the character of his God? The question shifts from one whose answer Job would never be able to comprehend—"Why did this happen?"—to one that only Job could answer: "Who do you believe God is?"

This reframing offers a model for us all: Here is a question we all must ask to make sense of the hard parts of our stories. It is a question my forebears cannot answer for me. I must wrestle with it myself in the present amid the sorrow of the losses in my family story and in my own life.

But I do not wrestle alone. The angel who explained to Joseph why the virgin Mary, his betrothed, was pregnant quoted a messianic prophecy given to the Old Testament prophet Isaiah seven centuries earlier that said, "The virgin will conceive and give birth to a son, and they will call him Immanuel (which means 'God with us')" (Matthew 1:23, quoting Isaiah 7:14). To be with us wholly, the Creator of all subjected himself to creation. From zygote to the cross, the beloved Son was at once fully human and fully divine. He inherited from his mother's line her DNA, the imprint of trauma's history on this family, a royal lineage, and a living, obedient faith. Those who recognize him as Son of God might add that Mary's son looks just like his Father (Colossians 1:15–6). Elsewhere in the book of Isaiah, we learn that this promised Messiah carries the grief of the generations in his body (Isaiah 52:13–53:12).

Throughout the ministry of Jesus recorded in the Gospels, he responded with incredible compassion to those who were suffering—whether from spiritual oppression, physical infirmity, or the searing sorrow of death. As I've sought to translate the trauma in my own family story, I've found solace in knowing that this compassionate Jesus is near to the brokenhearted. Because he is near, I maintain hope that trauma will not have the final word in our family stories: "Look! God's dwelling place is now among the people, and he will dwell with them. They will be his people, and God himself will be with them and be their God. 'He will wipe every tear from their eyes. There will be no more death' or mourning or crying or pain, for the old order of things has passed away" (Revelation 21:3–4). Then we will have the answers we need, even for the questions that seemed unanswerable in this lifetime.

Reflect

1. If your family story contains the story of a heroic forebear who overcame great odds, consider the trauma that this forebear might have undergone as part of their journey in life. What insights does this give you about the experiences of this forebear's immediate descendants?

2. Are there health or emotional patterns in your family that might be connected to inherited trauma?

3. As you consider the topic of trauma, what questions do you want to ask God? What does the descriptive identifier for Jesus, "God with us," mean for you as you seek to make meaning out of your family's history of pain?

FIVE

Patterns and Promises

Identifying the Consequences of Our Forebears' Decisions

M
Y CHILDREN ARE experiencing the effects of my grandfather's sins." Deborah[1] paused, then added, "But his
sins don't get to have the final word in my kids' lives. Or mine."

Deborah's grandfather was a missionary living a radioac-
tive double life. He raped his two daughters at frequent inter-
vals throughout their childhood. One of those daughters
—Deborah's mother Eleanor—tried telling her own mother
what her father had been doing to her. Eleanor's mother
didn't believe her.

"It was her mother's disbelief that multiplied the damage
of the incest," Deborah said. Eleanor was hospitalized for her
first nervous breakdown at age nineteen and received electro-
shock treatment to stabilize her and send her back into the
world. Shortly after Eleanor was released from the psychiatric

hospital, her father encouraged her to marry a young protégé of his. Douglas was an aspiring preacher. Perhaps Eleanor dreamed that Douglas would be her knight in shining armor and rescue her from the horrors of her childhood. But the fragile young woman would soon discover that Douglas was simply another version of Eleanor's father—an abusive narcissist who cloaked his toxic behavior in a veneer of spiritual activity.

After Eleanor gave birth to Deborah, she had her second major breakdown and was institutionalized for several months. A family in Douglas's church took care of the newborn for the first four months of her life until Eleanor was stable enough to return home. Douglas told everyone at church that Eleanor had been in the hospital for some physical issues, a lie he'd use again and again throughout the years every time he had to check her into a psychiatric hospital. The truth was that Eleanor had been diagnosed with schizophrenia.

Deborah's younger sister was born two years later, and the family of four lived a vagabond existence. "My dad moved us from place to place, starting new churches. When the elders he'd appointed to help run the congregation would begin to ask questions about our family's chaotic home life, he'd suddenly 'feel a call' to relocate," she said. "I lived in thirteen different homes, seven different states, and four different countries by the time I turned eighteen."

When she was stable, Eleanor worked as a nurse to provide for the family since Douglas's church work brought in little regular income. But she cycled in and out of psychiatric hospitals throughout Deborah's childhood. Douglas's grandiose ministry ambitions and constant cultivation of new donors and members meant that Deborah and her younger sister were frequently left to fend for themselves. "I remember being left alone by my parents for hours in run-down hotel rooms in strange towns from the age of five or six to care for my younger sister while my dad preached in churches on his circuit," Deborah said. "I learned early that my family's survival meant I could never, ever talk about what our home life was like—how often we moved, why my mom didn't get out of bed for weeks on end, and what it was like living with my pompous, verbally abusive father."

When Deborah was in her teens, her mother had a particularly serious psychotic break one morning when Douglas was out of town. To flee the voices that were tormenting her, a naked Eleanor ran into the street. Deborah had to chase Eleanor down, attempt to subdue her, get her back home, medicate her, and put her to bed. "I remember making school lunches for my sister after that, and we boarded the bus like it was any other day," Deborah said.

Her father insisted that Deborah enroll in his denomination's Bible college, and she planned to transfer to a state university as soon as she could convince him to allow her to do so. But while she was at the Bible school, she met some women who seemed to model a healthier version of the faith her father preached. Deborah committed her life to Christ, and vowed she'd live a different life than the one her parents had given her. Bible school seemed to offer her the formulas she'd need to solve the painful, turbulent puzzle of her family of origin.

Deborah married a Christian man nearly her father's age, and was full of hope that she was going to start a new chapter in her family's story using the formulas for a happy, healthy life she'd learned at Bible school. It didn't take long for the newlywed to realize that the formulas were no match for the generational patterns that had shaped her life. She'd married what was familiar to her. Her husband was an aloof father figure who was a combination of Eleanor's inability to parent her and Douglas's manipulative, selfish ways. Though Eleanor never spoke about the abuse she'd experienced during her own childhood, she communicated aversion to any form of sexual expression to her daughters. Deborah realized she'd carried not only her Bible school promises but also her parents' relational baggage into her marriage.

Dedicated to the hope her faith script promised, Deborah gave birth to two sons with her husband. It was the birth of those children and the powerful desire to nurture and protect them that brought Deborah to a crisis point in her life. In light of her mom's continuing descent into schizophrenia and her dad's ongoing cruel patterns of starting and then destroying or abandoning churches, Deborah realized that she needed more than formulas—even ones rooted in sincere Christian faith—to name and change generational patterns. Since then, God has used a small community of praying friends with whom she can be completely honest and a skilled counselor to help her recognize and break those patterns.

Real-life horror movie?

The host of the Food Network renovation show *Restaurant: Impossible*, Robert Irvine, leverages his military background and take-no-prisoners approach to diagnose and attempt to remediate the issues plaguing troubled restaurants. It doesn't take long for Irvine to expose the roots of those problems. Many of the small businesses featured on the show have dysfunctional family dynamics, poor cooking, or weak business skills fueling their failures.

A 2021 episode featured the story of a struggling soul food eatery tucked into a residential neighborhood in Buffalo, New York. The owners of the Park Vue restaurant were deeply invested in creating a hub to welcome and nourish the community they loved. But one of the owners, Schenita Williams, suggested that the challenges in their South Buffalo neighborhood had spiritual roots in the form of long-standing generational curses. Though Irvine seemed unfamiliar with the term, he suggested that Williams reach out to the many churches in the area in order to both strengthen community and market the restaurant.

The language of "generational curses" might sound to some modern ears like a plot twist in a 1950s horror movie, but the concept is found in the Bible. There has in recent years been a stream within the church that has given a whole lot of unhealthy attention to helping adherents identify and revoke specific generational curses as a subset of an emphasis on engaging in spiritual warfare.[2] That focus carries with it a temptation for some to view humankind as helpless victims of evil, and to think of God and Satan as equal opponents in a heavenly cage match. This kind of thinking is steeped in error and diminishes the victory over sin already won for each one of us through the life, death, and resurrection of Jesus.

With that in mind, those committed to translating the past benefit greatly from a healthy understanding of the generational consequences that may flow from the vows and choices made by our forebears. That understanding can help decode perplexing patterns and develop empathy for our family and for ourselves.

Several places in Scripture describe how the consequences of a parent's choices are passed on to subsequent generations.

The first commandment uses this kind of language when speaking about idolatry: "You shall not bow down to them or worship them; for I, the LORD your God, am a jealous God, *punishing the children for the sin of the parents to the third and fourth generation of those who hate me, but showing love to a thousand generations of those who love me and keep my commandments*" (Exodus 20:5–6, italics mine).[3]

The proportions in this passage highlight God's infinite compassion as well as God's perfect justice. "To the third and fourth generation" is a Hebrew-language idiom that means, roughly, "for as long as it takes."[4] God's justice is grounded in God's forgiveness and mercy for each one of us (James 2:12–13). Eugene Peterson's paraphrase of 2 Corinthians 5:15 in *The Message* says it well: "He included everyone in his death so that everyone could also be included in his life, a resurrection life, a far better life than people ever lived on their own." The cross demonstrates the contrast between the destructive consequences of sin in our lives and God's desire to redeem and restore.

The Bible's narrative contains descriptions of familial, rhyming rhythms of sin, such as the deceptions and favoritisms repeated in the lives of Abraham, Isaac, and Jacob. It also reveals that every generation is not shackled to the sinful decisions of the previous one. King Manasseh was an idolater, as was his son Amon. Yet Amon's son Josiah was a spiritual reformer, and under his leadership, the nation of Israel returned to worship of the one true God. After Josiah's death, sadly, Josiah's son Jehoahaz chose to return to the idolatrous ways of his grandfather and great-grandfather (2 Kings 21–23).

In a discussion about generational sin, one commentator notes:

God does not punish a new generation for the sins of a former generation. But God does hold accountable children who don't learn from their parents' mistakes. It is the responsibility of every generation to not repeat the mistakes of those that came before them. . . . When we observe brokenness within our families and choose a different path, one that aligns with God's redemptive plan for humanity, we can see clearly the loyal love of God.[5]

We are not responsible for the sins of our parents, grandparents, or great-grandparents, though we live with the consequences of their choices. For example, without intervention, patterns of abuse can repeat from parent to children to children's children.

Even so, writer Arah Iloabugichukwu challenges the sense of powerlessness some have when considering the curse-like and repetitive nature of destructive family and societal patterns:

There's a level of victimhood implied by the very idea of generational curses that renders us helpless to control our circumstances—a notion that isn't supported in the Bible or in any other religious text, for that matter. . . . The inability to envision a better future for oneself or the belief that the future is at the mercy of some grandfathered guilt leads to feelings of hopelessness, stagnancy, and depression, all of which decrease the likelihood that you do anything to change your circumstances. And, when the circumstances don't change, you point to the "curse" as the cause while unknowingly reinforcing the problem behavior for witnessing generations. If there is a curse, it's the one we cast every time we deny our ability to change the trajectory of our lives.[6]

God isn't asking us to pull ourselves up by our bootstraps with grit and gumption in order to change the trajectory of our lives any more than God is calling us to undergo a detailed exorcism-like renunciation of the sins of our great-great-grandparents so we can be free of the past. What is essential to the translator's task is an awareness of the gravitational pull that generational patterns and consequences may have in our lives. It's important to note that negative consequences are not the only thing that carries from one generation to the next.

This is best illustrated by the instructions God gave to the chosen people as they reached the end of their forty years of desert wandering and prepared to enter the Promised Land. Deuteronomy 28 spells out a list of consequences for either obeying or disobeying God's good commands. But it also offers a list of blessings that would flow out of the people's obedience. A blessing is an expression of approval and bequeaths to the recipient protection or favor. God wanted His people to know that there would be positive consequences for them, including the gifts of children, productive livestock and crops, protection from enemies, a place of respect among the other nations, and prosperity (vv. 1–14). The list of negative consequences flips this script with specific and vivid description of what they could expect if they chose as a people to disconnect from God (vv. 15–68).

In the context of a family, a blessing from parent to child can be far more than a well-wish or a greeting card sentiment. It can play a role in shaping that child's future.

Genesis 27 describes the way second-born twin Jacob (with the help of his mother Rebekah) stole the blessing his aging father Isaac intended to give to his firstborn son, Esau. Jacob received the prayer of blessing for abundance and a place of authority in both the family and the larger world (vv. 28–29). Those words of blessing had spiritual authority to them. This is why when Esau realized that his brother had taken that blessing from him and begged his father for a blessing of his own, Isaac could not say "Ditto for you to what I already prayed for your brother." Esau instead heard that he would live a difficult, violent life and would eventually throw off the authority his younger brother was given over him (vv. 39–40).

Some of you reading these words may feel that you've not received a blessing from your parents, whether because of their silence or via their expressed disapproval of the choices you've made. It can be a helpful reorienting exercise to recognize that God is the ultimate giver of every good gift, and desires to bless you in the context of the relationship you share. While consequences may be a part of our experience, God's foundational desire is in love to bless to a thousand generations—including the one in which we're living right now.

I will never ever

A related way that past consequences intersect with our present-day experience may occur in the form of a vow. The promises we make to ourselves, about ourselves or others, can form our identity in profound ways. Excavating the vows we've made to ourselves can uncloud our understanding of our story, bringing sunlight to the shadows in our work of translation.

A vow is a sacred and binding promise that is made between two parties without compulsion, and carries consequences if the pledge is broken. Perhaps most familiar to many of us are the "I do"s in a marriage ceremony, but all legal agreements are formalized vows. Though not all vows are inherently spiritual in nature, the Bible's guidelines about vows have contributed to our modern legal understanding about how these commitments are meant to function in society.[7]

In addition to legal covenants, most of us are shaped by the personal inner vows we make along life's way. Some of these vows may be positive: "I will stop smoking on January 1," "I will lose ten pounds," or "I will watch less television and read more books." Other vows may seem harmless: "I will eat one bite of this brownie. Wow, that brownie is pretty good. Maybe what I should have said was, 'I will eat this whole brownie.'"

But some of our vows may be a response to hurt, suffering, or abuse. "I must look perfect," "I won't let anyone know the real me," or "I will never be like my father." Writer Arlene Lageson defines an inner vow as "a binding promise made to oneself that shouts NEVER AGAIN as a result of a threatening or traumatic life event."[8]

I saw firsthand how powerful an inner vow could be. My mom first made a vow as a child that would direct her life. She grew up in a home with an unpredictable alcoholic father who let her know throughout her childhood in not-so-subtle ways that he didn't want her, though it would be years before she understood why. She learned to steel herself against the rejection she sensed with a promise she made to herself never to let anyone get too close to her. She rejected them before they could reject her. That childhood vow was sealed in cement after she found her parents had hidden the fact that she was adopted until they were forced by her birth father to reveal the truth shortly before she got married.

As a result, my mother viewed unforgiveness as a virtue and a source of protection in her life, which made my childhood home feel very unsafe for me. I sensed that if I crossed my mom, I would end up on her long "Never Forgive" list. As I write in my book *If Only: Letting Go of Regret*, "I spent my childhood doing what I could to hide from my mom's acid words. There was nothing more that I craved than forgiveness; it was how I experienced love. While I often found myself frustrated that my dad didn't do more to protect my sister and me from my mom's hurtful words, his affection for us was an antidote to some of the emotional toxins swirling around our home."[9]

When I was a teen, I came to faith in Jesus through the patient witness of a high school friend. Though I struggled to comprehend a forgiveness that wasn't tainted with generational pain and meted out by the milliliter, God's patient love held and protected me as I learned to walk with him. My vow to follow Jesus the Jewish Messiah was a declaration that I wanted to follow him into a different kind of future than my childhood seemed to predict.

As the years passed, I began to put together some of the pieces of my family story. I saw the ways in which my mom's trauma was connected to the caustic vows that had shaped her life—and mine. My dad died of leukemia on his sixty-fourth birthday, and for the next ten years after his passing, my mom's self-protective bitterness was her closest companion. In 2007, my sister and I each got a call from our mom, summoning us to a hospital near her home in South Florida.

When we arrived, we learned that she had Stage 4 breast cancer that had spread throughout her body. She told us she'd known for at least two years that she had breast cancer but had chosen not to pursue treatment. She'd hidden her condition from her coworkers at the medical office where she worked, from her neighbors, and from us until she was weeks from the end.

The hospice team encouraged her to use her remaining time on earth to focus on making peace in her primary relationships.

I reached out to her biological brother to let him know she was dying. He flew in from New York to spend a day with her. Morty was nine years older than my mom. He'd grown up living with his father and among family after their mother died one week after giving birth to my mom. He had longed for a relationship with his baby sister all his life and tried periodically to connect with her after my mom learned the truth about her origins, but her bitterness had always kept him at a distance. And she couldn't drop those old defenses during that final visit with her brother. "She's a hard one," Morty told me with tears in his eyes as he prepared to say goodbye.

Our conversations shifted after that in her last days. As she inched closer to the end, one of her Jesus-following hospice nurses invited my mom to talk to God with the two of us. I could scarcely believe my ears as I listened to my mother surrender to God and receive God's forgiveness. She died days later, released from the shackles of a vow that had held her throughout her life.

What is true?

As we assess the effect of consequences and vows from one generation to the next, we must begin by recognizing that in most cases, we don't have insight into our forebears' thoughts, nor were we direct witnesses of the circumstances surrounding their choices. We can't know how they decided what to eat for breakfast on March 4, 1881, much less the complex ways in which they approached decisions with larger import. And the consequences and vows of those further back in our family line are usually even more obscure. Translating the past includes reflecting on both the generational consequences of our forebears' choices and the personal vows we may have made. As we do, it's important to place those reflections in context of the other threads that go into creating our family story—especially trauma and the effect of larger cultural, subcultural, and historical pressures and trends at play during our ancestors' lives.

In Deborah's case, those cultural and historical pressures included the stigma of mental illness that resulted in silence and shame around her mother's schizophrenia, and the subcultural pressures included a church world that celebrated dynamic religious performance, thus rewarding her father's narcissism. Her parents carried with them the consequences of their own forebears' decisions and vows, their lives planted in soil that was fertile breeding ground for deep dysfunction. Deborah's translation task has included naming her own trauma and recognizing how those cultural and subcultural pressures and trends contributed to the iron-fisted vows her mother and father each made. She has also had to cross-examine the way these consequences have played out in her own life and has come to recognize that many of the vows she made as a child in order to seek control in the chaos and avoid telling the truth have had negative effects in her adulthood.

Negative consequences and vows are most often rooted in some form of a lie. In the final days of my mom's life, I saw firsthand how the lies her adoptive parents told her, withholding information about her family of origin and communicating that she wasn't fully welcome in this world, contributed to the belief that she couldn't trust anyone to keep her safe. Instead, she learned to protect herself via unforgiveness.

An accurate translator is able to convey meaning in a manner that is faithful to what has been expressed by the speaker and understandable to the hearer. In other words, translation of the past must be rooted in truth.

We need accurate information about our history, as much as we can reasonably gather, but we also need to interpret that information through the lens of unchanging truth. The facts of our family story may detail a long chain of sinful actions made by those who came before us, with incredibly painful consequences that continue to echo in our own lives. But the facts alone do not help us understand truth. Understanding the truth calls on us to make moral and ethical judgments about the past. It requires us to be honest about naming sin where it has existed in our forebears as well as in our own lives. Sin lies to us about who we are and who God is, distorting our ability to make sense of what the past is telling us.

Scripture is unflinching in what it says about the character trait of honesty, a reflection of God's own all-encompassing truthfulness. The ninth commandment (Exodus 20:16) is a prohibition against giving false testimony against another person—in other words, lying. Jesus not only claimed to be pure in his truthful speech, but personified truth itself with his divine claim in John 14:6: "I am the way and the truth and the life. No one comes to the Father except through me." Relationship with him will illuminate how we approach the subject of consequences and vows in our own family story.

An account from John 9 illustrates this. In it, Jesus and his disciples walked past a beggar who had been born blind. His disciples operated with the assumption that someone was to blame for the man's blindness. They asked Jesus whether the blindness was (a) a generational curse in action, or (b) a result of this man's sinful choice.

Jesus answered (c)—none of the above. Instead, he told them, "Neither this man nor his parents sinned . . . but this happened so that the works of God might be displayed in him" (John 9:3). Jesus went on to heal him, and in the wake of this miracle, the Pharisees sent for the man's parents and then the man in order to question them about this unprecedented turn of events.

The man's parents were intimidated by this ad hoc kangaroo court and told the Pharisees to ask their adult son to answer for himself. With a clear-eyed gaze, the healed man saw the Pharisees for who they really were and called them on it, then proclaimed his allegiance to his Healer. Rather than rejoicing in this miracle, the Pharisees focused their attention on the man, pronouncing him guilty of being born blind because of his own sin. Jesus told the Pharisees that his life would give sight to the blind and would blind the seeing. They responded with indignance, asking him if he was calling them blind (John 9:39–40).

His response revealed the truth about them: "If you were blind, you would not be guilty of sin; but now that you claim you can see, your guilt remains" (John 9:41). Our own biases and presuppositions and the set of negative consequences and vows based on lies that we may have inherited can obscure a clear view of the facts. Jesus will work with us to reveal the truth.

As is the case with so many other things, even the amazing "ah ha!" of a revelation is followed by the work of learning a new way to live in light of that truth. The man born blind had a lifetime of experience living in the darkness. Even after he could see, he had to learn new ways of working, worshiping, and interpreting the world around him. However, he didn't do so alone, but as a friend and follower of Jesus.

Unraveling generational consequences and vows is best done from a posture of asking, "What is true?" Some may find God uses the care of wise friends, insightful pastors or spiritual directors, or professional counselors to help answer that question. And all may discover that sometimes, we're too quick to fill in the blanks with *a* or *b*, when the truth is *c*, an expression of ongoing healing and repair in your family's story to the glory of God.

Reflect

1. What repeating patterns can you observe in your family's history? How have those patterns affected your life?

2. Are you aware of vows you've made in your own life? Can you identify what precipitated those vows?

3. Review the account found in John 9. Imagine for a few moments that you're the blind man in this story. What questions might you have had about your blindness in the years before you encountered Jesus? What message might you have had after your encounter with Jesus when you met others who were born with a disability?

SIX

Filling In the Blanks

Listening to the Mysteries in Our Family Narrative

NINE-YEAR-OLD Edward and his mother Betty were left alone in a world at war when John's father Richard abandoned the family in 1943.[1] Though Richard accused Betty of infidelity, he remarried weeks after the acrimonious divorce was finalized, and disappeared almost entirely from his son's life from that point forward. Edward found out what was happening in his father's life not because they spent time together, but via snatches of conversation between his mother, her few friends, and her lawyers surrounding the child support Richard refused to pay.

The young man lost not only his father, but also his only connection to his extended family of grandparents, aunts, uncles, and cousins. His mother's small family had scattered far and wide. As a result, Edward spent his childhood fending for himself. Betty worked long hours as a secretary for a rail-road and struggled with clinical depression, even spending a few months in a psychiatric facility at one point. She shipped Edward to military school while she was hospitalized because there was no one she could rely on to care for her only child.

Edward married when he was in his early twenties. He continued to be dutiful in his relationship with his mother, and had a handful of stiff, formal phone calls or visits with his father until Richard's death at age seventy-one when Edward was thirty-eight years old.

Richard had given Edward a last name that he could trace back through many generations. As he researched his family history, Edward learned that some of his forebears had come over before the American Revolution from landed gentry in Europe. A few years before his own death, Edward compiled his lifelong genealogical research for his children and grand-children into a thick binder filled with photocopied ship manifests, birth and marriage records, addresses, copies of deeds, and more.

A single page captured the story of a deeply broken rela-tionship between Edward and Richard. It was a copy of Richard's last will and testament. Richard had left his only child a dollar.

Richard's will was a commentary on the years of bitter battle with his ex-wife over child support payments as well as his cold, cruel character. Perhaps he imagined that when he left his family, he'd be able to cut his ties with them. But it seemed he lived the rest of his life with a spiritual version of phantom limb pain, which can happen in the wake of an amputation. The limb may be gone, but the nerve endings continue to send fiery pain signals to the brain as if the limb were still there. Richard's final words to his son were meant to hurt and punish in one final attempt to cauterize his own pain. According to one of Edward's sons, those words left an unhealed wound in Edward that ached throughout the rest of his life.

The sounds of silence

Edward's genealogical research traced one thread of his history. But as important as that thread was, it highlighted only one dimension of his complicated family story. His fractured relationship with his father was intertwined with that thread, as were the stretched, strained silences surrounding his mother's breakdown. Sensitive translators recognize that their role isn't to dissect and separate those tangled threads, but to recognize the patterns woven into the threads. Those looking to tease meaning from the past must learn to pay attention to the gaps, breaks, and silences in our family stories.

The effect of those interruptions in communication are illustrated in a lighthearted 2021 cellular network advertisement featuring music stars Gwen Stefani, Adam Levine, and Blake Shelton. California pop star Stefani tells Levine she's ready to begin a new romantic relationship and gives him a list of the qualities she's looking for in a partner: "I'm looking for someone completely different, maybe from another country, someone cultured and sensitive and not threatened by a strong confident woman." Because of spotty reception, all Levine heard from Stefani's message was "I want someone . . . country, . . . uncultured, and . . . threatened by a strong confident woman." Cue blue-collar Oklahoma country music personality Shelton, who enters the scene as if he's being fixed up by Levine on a blind date with Stefani. (As of this writing,

Shelton and Stefani, who are two costars on the music competition show *The Voice*, have married.) The cellular company wanted to use a bit of humor to show viewers that gaps in communication can have real-life consequences.[2]

When it comes to our family stories, those consequences often aren't quite so lighthearted. A failed family business can sever once-close sibling relationships. One generation of family members no longer gathers for holiday gatherings, and sees each other only when facing each other in courtrooms and lawyers' offices. The next generation doesn't know each other at all. Or a person with a long-standing addiction or untreated mental illness may spend a lifetime estranged from family. The empty chair waiting for that person at the holiday table is eventually put away for good as the years turn into decades.

While you may not be able to climb into the hearts of your predecessors who divided from one another, or to understand all the reasons for the estrangement, the concept of negative space can help you discover meaning in the silence and shadows where the story seems to stop.

Negative space is a term used in art and design. It is, simply, the space between things. The margins of this page, the white space that creates background and breathing room between each word, and the empty middle of round letterforms like *o* and *q* are all examples of negative space. Design blog *Framer* explains the importance of negative space in design: "On its own, negative space is nothing; it exists only in relation to positive space. You can only have a background if there is a foreground. You only get a hole because there is a form. You only see a gap because there are distinct objects."[3] Good design includes negative space as though it is in dialogue with its positive, expressive elements.

Genealogist Sophie Kay notes that negative space can illuminate what we do know about our family stories:

> In genealogy we are rarely gifted a continuous chronology for any ancestor. Instead we find ourselves piecing together their story from a series of discrete points in time. These dots of documentary evidence on a timeline eventually yield an impression of their life. Only by acknowledging the limitations of those individual points in time can we appreciate what each is contributing to the narrative.
>
> If you try to interpret the information you have without accounting for what you haven't yet searched for, you lack the context to make fair judgments of the evidence. Active use of the negative space in your tree and timelines can completely reshape your perception of the narrative.[4]

Divorce and estrangement aren't the only factors that can insert negative space into the timeline of a family. Other contributing factors might include

- Addiction

- Abuse

- The death of an elder who had been a connection point for gatherings and communication among extended family

- Deep division around topics such as politics, religion, childrearing practices, sexual orientation, or relationship choices

- Financial battles

- Gradual drift as members of the family relocate to new cities and let relationships go dormant

- The mists of history: the further back in time you go, the less information you may be able to access

Negative space can frame changes in family structure because of remarriage or cohabitation. If you're of a certain age or watched a lot of reruns of 1970s sitcoms at some point in your childhood, you probably remember the story of the second marriage of single parents Carol and Mike, whose family comprised her three daughters and his three sons. (Mike was a widower, and the original show never directly indicated whether Carol was divorced or widowed.) *The Brady Bunch* gave America an idealized look at the life (and groovy 1970s wardrobe) of a blended family. Blended families are created when one or both adult partners in a relationship have children from a previous relationship.

The show reflects a cultural shift as the long-held stigma around divorce and remarriage rapidly loosened. In 1960, 87 percent of American children were living in a two-parent household. The overwhelming majority of those households were first marriages for both parents. By the time *The Brady Bunch* went off the air in 1974, 70 percent of children were living in a two-parent household.[5] Today, more than a third of children under age eighteen are living with one parent.[6]

A 2015 Pew Research Center survey describes the changing face of the American family:

Not only has the diversity in family living arrangements increased since the early 1960s, but so has the fluidity of the family. Non-marital cohabitation and divorce, along with the prevalence of remarriage and (non-marital) recoupling in the U.S., make for family structures that in many cases continue to evolve throughout a child's life. While in the past a child born to a married couple—as most children were—was very likely to grow up in a home with those two parents, this is much less common today, as a child's living arrangement changes with each adjustment in the relationship status of their parents. For example, one study found that over a three-year period, about three-in-ten (31%) children younger than 6 had experienced a major change in their family or household structure, in the form of parental divorce, separation, marriage, cohabitation or death.[7]

A *Wall Street Journal* report on stepfamilies notes that it can take about ten years for a stepfamily to build lasting family bonds.[8] Today's fluidity in family structures and living arrangements suggests that a measure of these relationships may not endure long enough for enduring bonds to be created. While disrupted or changing family relationships often carry the grief of loss, they also carry hope and possibility for growth as new family groupings are created.

A sensitive family storyteller will recognize that in earlier generations, both blended families and single-parent households were often stigmatized by society. Stigma pushes people out to the margins and into the shadows. A family storyteller's attention can serve to destigmatize the past, even if much of that past remains hidden in the shadows.

I had an extended conversation not long ago with an older woman whose parents divorced in the 1940s, around the same time that Edward's did. She described the shame she felt throughout her childhood about the structure of her family, as so many in her community acted as though divorce were a contagious virus they were afraid of catching. She told me she learned to change the subject or lie about her parents' marital status when the topic of family came up with her friends at school. Though decades of social change have changed the way we talk about divorce, my friend confessed that she still struggled to talk about her own childhood because of the old scars left by the shame she once felt. She'd had decades of practicing that shame, but she told me that at this late stage of her life, she is committed to sharing her story with her grandchildren. She wants to leave a hopeful legacy with them, and she said their curiosity about her life has shone a light on feelings she'd learned to hide in the shadows. Her story reminded me that a family storyteller's empathy, curiosity, and perspective can be a healing balm to those kinds of decades-old scars.

The same empathy, perspective, and understanding is required for those who are attempting to interpret today's fluid or nontraditional family arrangements. Interpreters must listen with faith, care, and sensitivity to both the silences and the story that is unfolding among their loved ones in real time.

Forced apart

Other gaps in family narratives are caused by external forces. For example, war or the effects of political unrest can separate families and communities.

We may be familiar with the twentieth-century wars we learned about in U.S. history books, such as World Wars I and II and the Korean, Vietnam, and Iraq Wars, but the past century also included dozens and dozens of other conflicts around the world. Those in America may be less familiar with events like the Franco-Syrian War (1920), the Brazilian Revolution (1930), the Huk uprising in the Philippines (1946–54), or the Western Sahara War (1975–91), but these conflicts and too many more ended thousands of lives and disrupted millions more.[9]

In addition to war, other genocidal "ethnic cleansings" have taken millions of lives and torn families apart. There is a long history throughout the Americas of the genocide of Indigenous peoples and the practice of slavery. The repercussions of both echo to this day. Contemporary history is marked by numerous large-scale genocides including the pogroms (forced expulsion of a particular ethnic group, typically describing the actions in Russia and Eastern Europe in the late nineteenth and early twentieth centuries against the Jewish people), followed by the Holocaust before and during World War II, the Armenian genocide that occurred during World War I, the hundred-day genocide in Rwanda in 1994, the actions against Bosnian Muslims during the Bosnian War (1992–95), and the Uyghur genocide that has been ongoing (as of this writing) in China since 2014.

Three of my four grandparents were forced from their homes in Eastern Europe as a result of pogroms. The classic movie *Fiddler on the Roof* portrays a sanitized musical version of these events. The reality was far more brutal, as Jewish people were subjected to beatings, rapes, and massacre, and entire villages were forced to flee with only what they could carry on their backs. More than two million Jews immigrated to the United States during these years.[10] The bulk of my family made it over piecemeal, but not everyone escaped. Those who couldn't get out were often swept up in the Holocaust, which followed on the heels of the pogroms. My own genealogical research led me to discover that some extended family members who didn't make it out of Eastern Europe during the early years of the twentieth century appear to have been lost in the Holocaust.

According to the United Nations, in 2019, the number of forcibly displaced people in this world was 79.5 million—1 percent of the world's population. Children account for 40 percent of that number. This figure includes 26 million refugees, 45.7 million internally displaced people, and 4.2 million asylum seekers.[11]

Some of those fleeing war, violence, and poverty have migrated to the southern border of the United States. Some have sought to cross without documentation and permission. Others have sought asylum in America. From 2017 to 2020, a policy meant to deter those without documentation from attempting to enter the country separated minor children from their parents at the border. More than four thousand families were affected.[12] Though most were eventually reunited, as of April 2021, about 10 percent were still separated.[13] Trauma led to these migratory patterns and has been compounded by this policy. It is entirely possible that some of these families may never be reunified.

But the tragedy of family separation is not limited to the United States. Less than a decade after civil war broke out in Syria in 2010, the United Nations reported that 6.5 million Syrians had been displaced within the country's borders, and another 5.6 million had sought asylum in other lands.[14] A 2019 Public Radio International story highlighted the plight of the Zydia family. Because of the war, the close-knit clan was now living in a total of six different countries. Hiba Zydia, her husband, and their two children found their way to Canada. She stays in touch with her extended family via social media and messaging apps but grieves that her children won't know any of them as they grow up. She said, "We've gotten to a point where I don't think a lot about it, because if I think about the matter . . . it's a bit hard to take it. We don't think about it anymore—enough, we left those days behind." Samer, another Zydia sibling now living in Lebanon, noted that even if all the relatives had the financial means to regather, the politics in each country where family members now live regarding immigration, asylum, and the war have made the idea of a reunion impossible to imagine.[15]

Even as the Zydias struggle to maintain connection across time and distance put between them through no desire of their own, gaps in the family story are beginning to form. Their weekly Friday meals are now a distant memory, and even gatherings among the extended family for life cycle events like births, weddings, and deaths are no longer possible.

One thing leads to another

The Bible includes numerous accounts of fractured families, but none capture the gaps caused by dysfunction and resulting in exile better than the account of David and his son Absalom. That ruptured relationship rippled into subsequent generations until the nation of Israel, which was, by design, a family of families, divided in two. And one of those severed branches was carried away and wholly subsumed into the life of another people group.

King David was no stranger to loss. He had already buried one child, the son born to Bathsheba after he'd forced himself on her. He then manipulated events so Bathsheba's husband was killed in battle and he could claim the widow for his wife. The Bible says of this episode in unadorned language that the thing David did displeased the Lord (2 Samuel 11).

Second Samuel 13–18 details what happened after this occurred. David had at least eight wives including Bathsheba.[16] Absalom was his third son. Absalom's older half-brother Amnon became obsessed with Absalom's sister Tamar. It didn't matter to Amnon that Tamar was his half-sister. He raped the young woman. There is no report in Scripture that David enforced any sort of consequence for Amnon's action. As father and king, it appears that David neglected his responsibility to address his son Amnon's wicked actions. Absalom let his rage simmer for a full two years before he decided to avenge Tamar by killing Amnon. He then fled north from Jerusalem to the distant city of Geshur.

David longed for his son, and after three years, sent an emissary to invite Absalom to return to Jerusalem. Absalom did return but was counseled to keep away from his father. He did so for an additional two years until the awkwardness of the arrangement wore on him. Absalom decided he'd take his chances and present himself to his father. His father welcomed him, and the two seemed to settle into a decent rhythm of life. Four more years passed without incident.

But the whole time, Absalom was quietly fomenting a rebellion against David. He asked his father for permission to return to Hebron, where he'd been born, so he could worship God. Once he got there, however, Absalom declared himself king, and prepared to go to war with his father. The grievance that Absalom had been nursing for years toward his father came to a head—quite literally. In the midst of the chaos of battle, Absalom's long hair tangled in a tree, and David's trusted advisor killed Absalom.

I can almost hear David's screams of anguish when he received the news: "O my son Absalom! My son, my son Absalom! If only I had died instead of you—O Absalom, my son, my son!" (2 Samuel 18:33). But this conflict didn't end the strife. The seeds of division would bear bitter fruit two generations later.

David's second son by Bathsheba, Solomon, would ascend to the throne after his father's death. He reigned for forty years. Shortly before Solomon's passing, a prophet told him that his kingdom would be divided because of the idol worship he'd permitted to saturate the culture (1 Kings 11:29–31). After Solomon's death, his two sons battled for their father's throne. The rivalry between Rehoboam, who'd been anointed as king, and Jeroboam, who believed the throne was rightly his, split the kingdom in two. Rehoboam retained leadership of the areas containing land allotted to the tribes of Judah and Benjamin, which contained the center of worship for the land, Jerusalem. Jeroboam ruled over the land allotted to the other ten tribes. Against God's command, Jeroboam established another center of worship for his people (complete with golden calves!) so they wouldn't feel the need to travel to Jerusalem to worship the one true God (1 Kings 12–14).

The northern kingdom now known as Israel, marked by incredible spiritual compromise, survived for approximately two centuries before being invaded by Assyria. The ten northern tribes were marched from their land, enslaved, and dispersed among the Assyrian people. Those who weren't killed were forcibly grafted into the family trees of other peoples.

The two tribes of the southern kingdom, now referred to simply as Judah, were preserved to some degree by the worship taking place in Jerusalem. However, they too were prone to idolatry, which eventually led to their conquest and captivity in Babylon before their miraculous return to the land seventy years later.

Among other things, this Old Testament narrative illustrates how division plays itself out over time. Subsequent generations affected by this story may not have been firsthand witnesses to the pain and friction that played itself out in the relationship between David and Absalom, but the negative space took on a life of its own, growing into a breach so large that eventually an entire limb comprising ten branches of the family tree was swallowed whole by it.

Conversing with the silence

A quote widely attributed to the Roman philosopher and politician Cicero says, "Silence is one of the great arts of conversation."

Translating the past requires us to listen with sensitivity to the negative spaces in our family's story. The silence is an important part of the conversation, even if we can't always understand what it is telling us. Unless we come from royalty or a long line of scrupulous diary writers, we will find that silence fills the space between any historical data points we may have about our ancestors, including dates for births, baptisms, marriages, real estate purchases, census records, and deaths. Conversing with that silence may mean remembering with respect the lives that came before our own. This might include visiting their gravesites, noting the details you do know about them in a written history of your family, and reflecting on how their very existence has contributed to your own. I appreciate the words of this prayer as I've considered the mystery of my own unknown ancestors: "May we learn from their wisdom, better understand the challenges of their time, and appreciate the life they have given us."[17]

For those who've had family scatter or divide within the past couple of generations, the silence may not invite the same kind of quiet reflection. Instead, you may find yourself asking questions into the hush: What was the makeup of the extended family—aunts, uncles, cousins, grandparents—two or three generations ago? When and to where did those relationships scatter? What do you know about the reasons? Paying attention to the movement of the past may give insight into the current configuration of relationships among those in your extended family.

It is worth pondering the nature of those negative spaces. So many fissures in families begin with hurt, confusion, or grief before hardening into a great divide. Sometimes it happens in an instant, with a packed suitcase, as it did for Richard, the man who left his wife and young son in the account at the beginning of this chapter. Other times, a slow drift apart turns into permanent disconnection.

Negative space can be a frame of sorts, highlighting how the present came to be. The gaps in the story are not the end of that story. Your very existence is a witness to that truth.

Reflect

1. Which divisions and silences in your family story most pique your curiosity? Do you have any clues about what led to those gaps?

2. Have you or your forebears been forced to flee an ancestral home? What were the circumstances surrounding this experience? When and where did they (or you) go? Was the entire extended family able to find safe haven in another country or countries?

3. As you reflect on the story of David and Absalom, how would you characterize Absalom's attitude toward his father in the wake of the rape of Tamar by her and Absalom's half-brother Amnon? Was there a point in the story when different choices by David or Absalom could have led to a different outcome between the two? If so, where?

SEVEN

For This Child I Prayed

Discovering the Blessings and Challenges of Adoption in a Family's Story

ARCHBISHOP DESMOND TUTU has said, "You don't choose your family. They are God's gift to you, as you are to them."[1] When God forms a family using the choices of both birth and adoptive parents, the translator's task requires sensitivity in seeking to understand how multiple family stories intersect and unfold.

Though there is no single, central clearinghouse for adoption statistics, current estimates suggest that 2 percent of children in the United States are adopted via private domestic or international adoption or out of the foster care system—about 1.8 million children. Those numbers don't include stepparent adoptions or informal caretaking arrangements created within extended families. About

40 percent of adopted children are of a different race, ethnicity, or culture from that of their adoptive parent or parents.[2]

Each member of the adoption constellation (birth parents, adoptive/foster/kinship caregiving parents, siblings, and people who are adopted) often faces complex emotions regarding the various interconnected relationships. Those emotions and the attendant questions of identity can surface throughout a lifetime. There is no one-size-fits-all formula that will allow you to interpret these stories as they continue to unfold in the lives of every member of the adoption constellation. But if adoption is a part of your family narrative, understanding the joys, challenges, and losses surrounding adoption can assist you in translating your story.

Adopted into new community

"I love my parents. I'm so glad they adopted me," Canadian pastor Anna Spray told me. "They were the parents God intended for me. I would not be who I am today without them."

Anna's mother and father each came from families where adoption was not only common but celebrated. "My mother was raised in a home where she was one of four children—three biological and one adopted sibling," she said. "My mom's dad was an Anglican priest, and throughout her childhood, the family provided foster care for many children. My father grew up in an environment where many in his family had pursued adoptions." Anna's parents dealt with infertility for many years and turned to adoption as another way to build their family. They first adopted Anna's sister, then Anna, then eventually had two biological children as well.

Anna said each child's unique origin story was honored in her family. "I've always known I was adopted, and our family always celebrated the days my older sister and I came home to be with them."

She noted that her family's congregation was an ongoing source of love and care for each one of them. "Our tight-knit church community was very supportive of all the ways God was growing our family. They had been praying for and with my parents for years and were deeply invested in our lives. They were like an extension of our family," Anna said.

Neither Anna nor her older sister ever felt particularly compelled to seek out their birth families. "Our birth parents were like imaginary friends, not real people," Anna said. "Because we were at home in our home, there was no longing to connect with them." However, when Anna was twenty-one, her grandmother urged her to reach out to see what she could learn. Anna exchanged letters with her birth mother and learned that she had been conceived because her birth mother had been raped. Anna was grateful her birth mother elected to carry her to term and place her for adoption.

"God is always for life," Anna said. "We need to expand our imaginations for redemption and restoration." She believes her very existence is a testimony to that reality.

Redemption and restoration

Redemption and restoration are reflected in the way the Bible describes adoption, and that foundation has shaped, albeit unevenly, our contemporary legal canon around the topic.

Though the Old Testament never uses the word *adoption*, God's work in creating new families for redemptive purposes is seen throughout its narrative. God chose the aging Abram to leave his family and become the patriarch of an entirely new nation that would be devoted to his service (Genesis 12:1–3; 7). Moses's mother, in a desperate attempt to save his life, entrusted her child to God by placing him in a tar-coated basket in the reeds along the Nile. In effect, Pharoah's daughter became the baby's foster mother (Exodus 2:1–10; Acts 7:17–22).

The book of Ruth opens with the account of a young Moabite woman who refused to go back to her home village after her husband died, clinging instead to her Hebrew mother-in-law Naomi and insisting that Naomi's people were her true family and Naomi's God was now her God (Ruth 1:15–18). Ruth's great-grandson King David wrote these words:

A father to the fatherless, a defender of widows,
    is God in his holy dwelling.
God sets the lonely in families,
    he leads out the prisoners with singing;
    but the rebellious live in a sun-scorched land.
(Psalm 68:5–6)

The New Testament uses the language of adoption, which was a part of the dominant Roman culture in the first century, throughout its texts as signifier of the kind of chosen-ness Jesus was offering Jews and Gentiles alike. Jesus told his disciples that he would not leave them orphaned in this world and would send his Spirit to teach and lead them (John 14:18). Paul uses the Greek word for adoption (*huiothesia*, which means "to place as a son") five times in the New Testament to highlight the way God creates a kingdom family.[3]

Throughout history, children whose parents have died or were unable to care for them have been raised by other families. Some received all the rights and responsibilities of an heir. Others were enslaved and were treated as property. In the United States, laws were enacted beginning in the mid-1800s that began to formalize the adoption process.

The University of Oregon's Adoption History Project suggests that the broad acceptance of adoption in the United States reflects core values like immigration and democracy that speak to the importance Americans have historically placed on shared purpose over inherited social or political privilege. Project researchers write, "Adoption has always had a symbolic importance that outstripped its statistical significance. Adoption has touched only a small minority of children and adults while telling stories about identity and belonging that include us all."[4]

Today, a statistical majority of the adoptions in the United States are adoptions by relatives or stepparents. However, since the end of World War II, international adoption has been on the rise. Transracial adoptions make up 44 percent of U.S. domestic adoptions. Most international adoptions pair children from Africa, Asia, and Central and South America, and create transracial families.[5] Experts at the Adoption History Project note, "Because growing numbers of adoptions are transracial and/or international, many of today's adoptive families have literally made adoption more visible than it was in the past."[6]

That visibility has been one component that has helped remove some of the secrecy around adoption that marked law and practice during most of the twentieth century. Many birth mothers desired to keep news of their pregnancies hidden from their families or communities, but not necessarily from the adoptive family and the child to whom they'd given birth. However, prevailing social wisdom was that the negative space of enforced secrecy was always the best for everyone involved, and that adoptive children would never be curious about their birth families. Laws and policies based on those assumptions were enacted during those years.[7]

Sealing adoption records is no longer the only option for birth and adoptive parents. Social mores have changed, as have attitudes about secrecy. At least 60 percent of adoptions today include some form of open adoption, which means there is some sort of disclosure of information between birth parents and adoptive parents.[8] This can range from unsealed files to occasional updates from adoptive parent to birth parent via letter or email to routine in-person visits.

In addition, a much richer understanding of the tasks and challenges faced by each member of the adoption constellation is challenging the way adoption was treated as recently as a couple of generations ago. Adoption is not a single event, or even a series of events, but a story that unfolds throughout the lifetime of each member of the constellation, and often echoes into subsequent generations.

The seven core issues of adoption

Beginning in the 1980s, the conversation around adoption began to change to one of greater openness and awareness that highlighted seven core issues affecting each member of the adoption constellation, as well as other stakeholders in the process, such as foster and extended family. The North American Council on Adoptable Children offers helpful descriptions of how each of these issues unfolds:

1. *Loss:* Adoption begins with "an initial loss and many secondary losses that continue to affect constellation members throughout their lives."

2. *Rejection:* The experience of rejection accompanies a "perceived loss of social acceptance, group inclusion, or a sense of belonging. Rejection can be real, imagined, or implied. People get their most basic needs met through human connectedness; being rejected or ostracized from a person, family, or community can leave an individual feeling a deep sense of abandonment and isolation."

3. *Shame and guilt:* "Rejection leads to feelings of shame and/or guilt. . . . Shame is the painful feeling that one is bad and undeserving of deep connections and happiness. Guilt is a feeling of responsibility or remorse for some offense, crime or wrong, whether real or imagined. Shame is about 'being' (I'm bad) and guilt is about 'doing' (I did something bad)."

4. *Grief:* Every member of the adoption constellation will face complex grief, "as they have experienced a profound loss that changed the trajectory of their life. In the re-arranging of family trees through adoption and permanency, parents are grieving unborn children, children are grieving as their understanding of what happened to them unfolds, and birth/first parents are grieving the loss of their baby/child that they hope is alive and well."

5. *Identity:* "All individuals are on a quest to understand who they are, where they fit, and to share their stories with others to better understand themselves. Stories that

are broken due to historical or personal events can make it difficult for people to understand and express who they are and solidify their life's narrative."

6. *Intimacy*: "If individuals have acknowledged their core losses, noted where, when and with whom rejection surfaces, addressed feelings of shame and guilt, taken time to grieve, and have embraced their identity, they are able to offer an authentic self in an intimate relationship. Identity and intimacy are linked; as a person clarifies and re-clarifies who they are, their ability to relate to others, forgive others, embrace others, and trust others is enhanced."

7. *Mastery and control*: "Unidentified, un-named, unac-knowledged and un-grieved losses can create intense feelings of powerlessness." All members of the constella-tion have at some point lost a sense of mastery over their life circumstances. "The ultimate goal for all members of the constellation is mastery, which is a regaining of a sense of authority and control." Mastery is a key compo-nent of emotional and spiritual resilience.[9]

This isn't to say that those involved in the adoption con-stellation face a diminished future. In fact, the vast majority thrive. But awareness of the unique set of ongoing tasks and challenges surrounding adoption can help clarify issues as they arise.

A landmark 2007 study compared the social and emo-tional well-being of adopted children to that of all children and found that 88 percent of adoptees age six and above exhibited positive social behaviors, in contrast to 94 percent of children in the general population. There were measurable differences when it came to emotional and behavioral challenges: 26 percent of adoptees ages six and up (versus 10 percent of the general population) were diagnosed with attention deficit disorder/attention deficit hyperactivity disorder, 9 percent of adopted children ages two and up (versus 4 percent of the general population) dealt with depression, and 15 percent of adopted children ages two and up (versus 4 percent of the general population) presented behavior conduct problems.[10]

Attachment issues are not at all limited to children in the foster and adoptive community. Any child who experiences abuse, neglect, or disruption during the early years of life may have difficulty forming trusting emotional bonds with caregivers and others. However, because of the circumstances that bring many children into the adoption constellation, there is today heightened awareness and education for families in the constellation regarding attachment.

Reactive attachment disorder (RAD) is a specific psychological diagnosis that describes the disconnected relationships and occasionally cold, cruel behaviors of some children at the far end of the attachment spectrum.[11] Fern and Tom[12] had talked to dozens of adoptive parents, taken classes, and read everything they could about adoption and the effects of institutionalization on child development before adding seven-year-old Hwan to their family. Little information was available to them about Hwan's early years. The orphanage in South Korea noted that he had some speech and cognitive delays and was quite small for his age, likely because of his malnourished state when he arrived at the orphanage between three and four years of age.

Fern and Tom prepared for Hwan's arrival into their family by assembling a team of doctors, therapists, and people who'd adopted internationally, and by creating connections with their local Korean community. They were as prepared as they could be, and they hoped that their love for him and the many years of prayer leading up to and continuing through his adoption would carry them through the challenges they knew lay ahead.

Even with all of those supports in place, Fern and Tom were often overwhelmed by the intensity of Hwan's angry outbursts, stealing, and lying. Early on, he received a diagnosis of RAD. As he approached his teens, Hwan grew more violent, and they discovered that he had been sexually abusing their newly adopted infant daughter. After exhausting several outpatient treatment options, they ended up placing their son in a long-term residential program. They see him often, and they believe he is making progress toward being able to function independently in society as he moves toward adulthood. It isn't how they dreamed things would go when they launched into the adoption process. They continue to grieve his complicated absence from their daily lives, but believe they are doing what is best for their whole family, including their beloved son.

On the language of "real" parents

"Are those your real *parents?"*

This insensitive question is one with which those in the adoption constellation must contend, and there is no formulaic answer, because there is no single definition of family.

Rhiannon[13] grew up in a home with parents who opened their doors to anyone who needed refuge. At one point, this included Rhiannon's birth mother, who lived with the family for a few months when Rhiannon was a preschooler. But she never told Rhiannon she was her biological parent, and Rhiannon's adoptive parents couldn't figure out how to tell their daughter the truth about the relationship.

"Throughout my childhood I had asked my parents multiple times if I was adopted," Rhiannon told me. "There were certain things that made me wonder: I had never seen a picture of my mom pregnant, both of my parents had blue eyes and I have brown ones, and my body type is different from everyone else's in my family. They always laughed and brushed off the question. I even told a teacher at my middle school that I was almost positive I was adopted."

Because of the ongoing relationship Rhiannon's parents had with her birth mother, they struggled to find a good way to tell their daughter the truth. "They didn't talk about it, because they were scared that I would be upset that they hadn't told me sooner, or that I would forget about them and try to only pursue my biological family," she said. "None of that happened. I was so happy they told me when I was thirteen. It made us grow closer. I don't stay in constant contact with my biological mother. I don't feel a need to do so, and she never tried to treat me like I was her kid. My biological father was out of the picture, and I have no desire to search for him."

Rhiannon's understanding of "real" family includes her birth mother and her extended family, but her roots are anchored deeply in her close, sprawling adoptive family.

Other adoptees have navigated the question of "real family" in different ways. Some choose to reserve the title of parent for their adoptive parents alone, as they're the ones who engaged in the day-in and day-out experience of raising the child. Other adoptees enfold their birth mother and father in their understanding of who their "real" parents are. There is no single answer to the question.

Honor thy parents?

If adoption is a part of your family story, translating the past requires a measure of functional fluency in adoption's history, tasks, and challenges. I've learned it also calls for sensitivity to the complex nature of all the relationships involved, as well as a recognition that there will likely be blank spaces in the narrative, as previously discussed in chapter 6.

Translating the past in a faithful way also calls for a generous understanding of how to heed the words of the fifth commandment: "Honor your father and your mother, so that you may live long in the land the LORD your God is giving you" (Exodus 20:12; cf. Deuteronomy 5:16).[14] The Hebrew word used for honor (*kabed*) comes from a root word meaning a heavy, great weight. It conveys that we're talking about something extremely important. *Kabed* is often used in reference to God's glory.[15]

The straightforward words of this command may leave some in the adoption constellation struggling to make sense of what this looks like in their context—especially if a birth or adoptive parent's abuse, neglect, or addiction was a part of the narrative. In cases like these, time spent with a counselor experienced in adoption issues can help adoptees or those in the constellation looking to support them begin to understand how to respond to God and their parents. The core tasks of adoption are amplified and distorted when there's been deep dysfunction.

Honoring parents begins with acknowledging their full humanity, recognizing that each came to the parenting task as the product of their own imperfect family histories. Their flaws and failures are not the sum of who they are. That said, healthy boundaries are an essential expression of *kabed*. Those boundaries may require distance from a toxic member of the constellation, not to try to outrun the pain of the past, but so that the work of translation can continue in a safe, supported environment.

For those pondering how to represent family stories that include adoption, a traditional family tree diagram presents a dilemma. Writer Kimberly Powell says, "Almost every adoptee, no matter how much they love their adopted family, experiences a twinge when faced with a family tree chart. Some are unsure whether to trace their adopted family tree, their birth family, or both—and how to handle the differentiation between their multiple families. Others, who for various reasons have no access to their own personal family history prior to their adoption, find themselves haunted—by the family whose names will never be documented in their genealogy, and the family tree somewhere in the world with an empty space on the branch where their name should be."[16] Appendix A offers some resources for those who are looking for creative ways to tell their family's adoption story in a visual manner.

The New Testament carries the reminder that *kabed* is meant to be a two-way street in families. After quoting the fifth commandment in his letter to the Ephesians, the apostle Paul adds this directive: "Fathers [or parents], do not exasperate your children; instead, bring them up in the training and instruction of the Lord" (6:4). The kind of exasperation to which Paul refers here is not gentle teasing, but the kind of provocation that leaves wounds and fractures community. The sensitive translator of the past will recognize that although opportunities for exasperation are multiplied in adoption, so too might be the possibilities for redemption and restoration.

It may seem counterintuitive to press into that sense of exasperation. Learning to face rather than flee from adoption's complex issues and relationships takes a tremendous amount of emotional energy. A willingness to persist—and to seek professional help if needed, as well as the support of a faithful praying friend or two—can move you toward a sense of wholeness, even if some (or all) of the relationships in an adoption constellation are fragmented or nonexistent.

Restoration isn't a happily-ever-after ending. Instead, it reflects the value of the ongoing process of learning a number of different vocabularies and dialects from all the voices in your constellation so you can discern the words that best tell your story.

Reflect

1. Has adoption been a part of your family story? If so, how? If not, what experiences have you had with the topic? What images from news, movies, or books do you carry on the subject? Do you know people who are a part of specific adoption constellations?

2. Though the trend today is moving away from sealed records and secrecy in adoption, are there times when this might be a better option?

3. When considering what Scripture has to say about adoption, what strikes you as you consider the relationship described in Romans 8:14–15 and the gifts and benefits of that relationship in Romans 8:38–39? (For those from difficult families, what does this passage have to say about your heavenly Father?)

EIGHT

Who Are My People?

Discerning How Race, Ethnicity, and Religion Shaped the Experience and Identity of Our Ancestors

THE COMEDIAN GROUCHO MARX was known for his quick-witted quips. One of his most famous was "Please accept my resignation. I don't care to belong to any club that will accept me as a member."

While we may sometimes wish we could resign our membership in the various "clubs" of which we are members, when it comes to our family histories that is typically not an option. Our histories make us automatic, lifelong members in various racial, ethnic, and religious groupings; we belong to many different circles. The interpreter's task includes a bit of armchair sociology and anthropology as we consider the implications of these memberships.

What are you doing here?

I took my two young grandsons to a local park in their city neighborhood on a postcard-perfect, warm, early summer morning. I chased the eighteen-month-old as he did a gleeful high-speed tour of the playground equipment. Within minutes, his six-year-old brother had already bonded with a brand-new pack of playground BFFs.

After a while, I coaxed the little one over to his stroller with the promise of a snack so I could take a quick breather before he launched again. I sat on the bench next to him, noticing for the first time a line of mothers clustered on a couple of benches across the park from me. They were scrutinizing my every move as they whispered among themselves. I wondered how long they'd been watching me.

I smiled and nodded in their direction, which unleashed another round of murmuring among the group. I turned my attention to my toddler grandson, wiping his laughing, sticky face. As I did, a little girl about the same age as my older grandson approached me. She put her hands on her hips, and said, "My mom wants to know what a white lady like you is doing here." She looked over her shoulder at the group on the bench.

It hadn't dawned on me until that moment that I was the only person on the playground who wasn't Hispanic.

"I'm an abuela," I said. "I'm a grandma, here with my grandsons," I said. I waved at my older grandson on the slide. Their father is from Mexico, and both boys resemble him. The little girl stood another moment, sizing me up like a veteran detective, then ran back to report to the mamas sitting on the bench on the other side of the park.

I understood their concern. No doubt they wondered as I was wandering the playground whether I was an agent from

Immigration and Customs Enforcement, or a cop, or maybe even a kidnapper. I gave the group a small wave and a smile as I scooped my beautiful brown grandbaby out of his stroller and set him free to run and play.

Seeing in living color

A good translator will seek to understand how race, ethnicity, and religious identity shape every family's experience. We may wish we lived in a world where those dividers don't exist, but attempting to ignore them mutes a good translator's ability to realistically interpret the past.

"'Race' and 'ethnicity' have been and continue to be used as ways to describe human diversity," said Nina Jablonski, an anthropologist and paleobiologist at the Pennsylvania State University. "Race is understood by most people as a mixture of physical, behavioral and cultural attributes. Ethnicity recognizes differences between people mostly on the basis of language and shared culture."[1]

Dr. Frederick Leong further illuminates the overlapping-yet-distinct nature of the categories of race and ethnicity, noting, "Racial identity is believed to emerge based on experiences with racism and oppression due to phenotypic differences, such as skin color or facial features. Ethnic identity, by contrast, is believed to develop from a more basic need to belong and identify with similar others."[2]

A sensitive explorer of family history will seek to understand those similarities and differences. The words of Chicago elementary school teacher Ashley McCall explaining why she can't claim colorblindness in her classroom are instructive to all of us learning to be translators:

As educators we must, to the best of our abilities, see our students, families, and neighbors in the fullness of their identities. Race may be a social construct, but it informs our students' day-to-day experiences: rides on the bus, walks to and through stores, drives down the Dan Ryan [Expressway], and kicking back in the park with friends. . . . To say, "I don't see race" is to say, "I don't see you. I don't know you. And I'm not ready and willing to hear and believe you." I do not know an educator that would ever say this to a student. But until all teachers are ready to see and explicitly engage with issues of race in the classroom, we are sending this harmful message subconsciously.[3]

In addition, racial and ethnic categories have shifted over time. Several generations ago, racial classifications were based on nationality, religion, or language. Immigrant Irish and Italians were once categorized as members of different races by white Americans who'd been living in the country for generations. Today, those groups are grouped as Caucasians with those who'd once classified them as "Other."

To further illustrate, Spanish speakers may share the same language (with many different accents!), but a dark-skinned Afro-Caribbean individual will have a very different experience in this country compared to a light-skinned person of Spanish and German parentage who is immigrating to the United States from Argentina. In twenty-first-century America, skin color is a principal way that we classify people by race.

JaeRan Kim was adopted from Korea and says that her white parents' colorblind approach to race in their family didn't prepare her for the challenges she'd meet as she moved into the adult world on her own: "As the only adoptee and person of color in my immediate and extended family, I was always assured my parents didn't see color and loved me no matter what, and that was enough. After going to college and being exposed to the racial and cultural diversity I had been missing growing up, I began to explore my racial identity and realized that for transracial adoptees, a parent's love and rejection of racial difference does not meet the need for racial, ethnic, and cultural identity development and support."[4]

Transracial adoptees aren't the only ones who find themselves on the cutting edge of questions about race and identity. According to a 2019 Kaiser Family Foundation survey, 2.9 percent of the U.S. population is biracial or multiracial, as my own grandsons are.[5] As America's demographics continue to change in the coming years, white people are expected to become a statistical minority by 2045.[6] Whether your family's story is based in a small farming community comprising the descendants of Norwegians who immigrated to the United States in the mid-1800s or whether you are a multiracial child navigating life in a large city, a translator's task includes recognizing how racial biases and strengths contribute to identity.

Lutefisk or lasagna?

My parents weren't particularly religious, and we were infrequent synagogue attenders, but I learned about my Eastern European Jewish racial and ethnic identity[7] through the foods we ate, the jokes we told, the holidays we celebrated, the holidays (like Christmas and Easter) that we *didn't* celebrate, and the experiences my parents recounted as they navigated a majority culture pockmarked with anti-Semitic words and attitudes.

Every one of us learns about our ethnic identity through family stories, meals, traditions, rituals, and gatherings, such as

- A lavish buffet filled with traditional Swedish foods on Christmas Eve

- A Greek Orthodox wedding

- Navajo (Diné) Blessingway ceremony

- Farsi spoken at home

- A quinceañera[8]

- A grandmother's special lasagna recipe

- Yearly trips to visit family in Taiwan

- Diwali celebrations with extended family and friends

- A week with relatives each summer at an old cabin full of memories and stories in northern Wisconsin

- Coming together for a family member's funeral

- Eid al-Fitr gatherings

- And, of course, those old stories families share when they gather

We learn about ethnic identity from our family of origin, both through casual family conversation and in the ways we mark milestones and holidays. We also catch instruction via our elders' attitudes toward other groups. It can be those points of contrast with others around us that do the teaching: Why does our family eat gefilte fish instead of lutefisk like the Nilssons?

Researcher Jean Phinney notes that ethnic identity comprises

- Ethnic awareness—understanding of one's own and other groups
- Ethnic self-identification—label used for one's own group
- Ethnic attitudes—feelings about one's own and other groups
- Ethnic behaviors—behavior patterns specific to an ethnic group[9]

Even those who don't claim a strong sense of ethnic identity but see themselves primarily as Americans are marked by regional identities and loyalties. You might eat a hot dog or two on Independence Day, but what brand of hot dog do you throw on your grill? And what are your preferred toppings? The "garden on a bun" hot dog beloved in my hometown of Chicago is not the sauerkraut-topped hot dog sold by street vendors in New York City.

The need to belong to a people is hardwired into us as humans. That need can bring us together or it can divide us. World history is marked by ethnically motivated attitudes and behaviors that have led to war and genocide. Understanding our family's past requires both a willingness to explore the implications of our ethnicity or ethnicities and a sober appraisal of how that history and identity has been experienced in the world. What biases and fears of other ethnic groups mark my family's history? Where has there been friction and hurt in the past between my ethnic group and others?

Faith communities

Another way we are shaped by group identity is via religious affiliation. Though the word *religion* may connote personal devotion and commitment, a good translator also recognizes that it also points to how people understand themselves as members of a group—even if they're not active adherents within that group. One writer notes, "Similar to other forms of identity formation, such as ethnic and cultural identity, the religious context can generally provide a perspective from which to view the world, opportunities to socialize with a spectrum of individuals from different generations, and a set of basic principles to live out. These foundations can come to shape an individual's identity."[10]

I've known many people who weren't practicing members of a particular faith tradition who still identified as members of that religion because their forebears were members. Others can point with pride to a long, unbroken chain of active faith engagement within their family. A translator of the past will recognize that religious identity is often transmitted from generation to generation while simultaneously recognizing that God has no grandchildren. Every new generation must connect with God afresh, Parent to child.

The power of religious identity can be seen most clearly when that identity shifts. When someone of one faith moves to another, family and community relationships are often strained or severed. And sometimes the decision to leave one faith for another can cost some adherents their livelihoods—or lives.

Mission organization Open Doors USA compiles data about persecution of Christians around the world. Of the top ten most dangerous countries in the world for a person to be a Christian, eight countries, including Afghanistan, Libya, Iran, and Nigeria, are majority Muslim; one (North Korea) is atheist; and one is majority Hindu (India).[11] Converting to follow Jesus in these countries is viewed as a betrayal of family and society. Even though conversion to Christianity is a capital offense in some Muslim countries led by hardliners, the longing for a different faith and life has fueled this movement for some from Islam to Christianity. David Garrison of the mission organization Global Gates discusses the phenomenon in a *Newsweek* op-ed: "No solitary factor could explain today's unprecedented turnings. Instead, it seemed to be a mélange of factors producing a climate ripe for large-scale and widespread conversions."[12]

A few years ago, I was asked to write some curriculum for Muslim children enrolled in a Christian faith-based after-school program. I was told to focus on telling Bible stories in a welcoming way so that children and parents alike could receive hospitality from the organization's staff in order to create meaningful space where families could explore questions about the two faith's similarities and differences. When I asked the director of the program what qualified me, a Jewish follower of Jesus, to create these materials, he smiled and said, "You love the Bible, and because of your Jewish heritage, you understand at some level the monotheistic faith within the Muslim community, and know the challenges that those coming to faith in Jesus will face in a way that many American Christians don't."[13] The staff desired to share their faith with sensitivity while taking every precaution to ensure that young children wouldn't be at risk of punishment at the hands of an angry family member if that child expressed an interest in knowing more about Jesus.

The director was aware that I'd faced a difficult experience in my home after I came to faith in Jesus when I was fifteen. Though my parents weren't especially religious, they saw my actions as traitorous. History is replete with the accounts of terrible things done to the Jewish people in the name of Christ, and I understood and empathized with my parents' deep hurt. Judaism is unique in the world in that it is an identifier of race, culture, and faith.[14] Losing connection with ethnic and religious community has often been the reality for Jewish people like me who have chosen to follow Jesus.

It is not just those who move from one faith to another who might experience exclusion, shunning, or persecution. A shift in religious identity can happen among those who move from one branch to another within the broader Christian tradition. For instance, if someone who grew up in a devout Catholic home becomes a member of a Mennonite church in adulthood, some in their family of origin may view this as a form of betrayal to the family or a step away from faith.

However, in the West, individualization of religious identity has led to more fluidity in religious affiliation—or non-affiliation—in the past couple of generations. Fewer people than ever are "inheriting" their religious affiliation from their forebears. Some families possess heirloom family Bibles dated with inscriptions of births, baptisms, marriages, and deaths, but these artifacts are increasingly rare in contemporary times.

Researcher Edward Queen II notes that for much of history, a person was born into a particular religion: "Religious identity was a social and cultural given, not a result of individual choice. It was given to an individual by external forces and actors, not chosen by the individual. Tolerance has become a social and moral value. This has resulted in a situation where, for most people most of the time, religious identity becomes nothing more than a privatized affair without deep connections to the historical traditions of the community of faith."[15]

Though religious identity has in some ways become a more individualized affair, involvement in faith communities still plays a significant role in shaping identity.

A safe place

Jenny's[16] faith community became her family when her biological parents abandoned her. "I grew up hearing from my parents that they didn't want me," she said. "They both had alcohol addictions. My dad was in and out of prison. My mom would leave us with various neighbors for weeks on end. And when they did take care of me, they mistreated me. This included everything from burning me with lit cigarettes to sexual abuse."

When Child Protective Services got involved, Jenny cycled between a series of foster homes and living with her parents. "I knew what it would take to survive staying with my parents, and even though it was a terrible situation, it was better than the unpredictable things I experienced in foster care," she said.

A girl named Maria Wilson befriended Jenny during her freshman year in high school. Maria began inviting Jenny to church events. Shortly thereafter, Jenny committed her life to Christ at one of those events. "Maria's dad picked me up for youth group every single week," said Jenny. "And as the family got to know me, they opened their home to me for meals. They gave me a safe place to stay whenever I needed it. As soon as I turned eighteen, they invited me to move in with them. I accepted immediately, and never returned to my birth parents' home again."

The Wilson family continually emphasized that their family was a part of a larger family—that of their local church. Jenny discovered a network of relationships in church that taught her what extended family could look like. The Wilsons enfolded her as one of their own, always giving her a place to call home throughout college and afterward. Jenny spends holidays with the Wilsons, and she calls Maria's parents "Mom" and "Dad."

A few years ago, Jenny discovered that her biological father had taken out a mortgage for himself using her identity. As part of untangling that financial and legal mess, Jenny sought a legal name change. With the family's blessing, she changed her last name to Wilson.

"I'm so thankful that the Wilsons showed me that family life doesn't have to be the biological mom-dad-kids of traditional Christianity. I'm thankful that family in the church is so much more than that," Jenny said. She has had no contact with her biological family for decades. Though she still feels deep sadness surrounding the messaging that she wasn't wanted by her family of origin, she has found a measure of healing through her relationship with the Wilsons, and through them, with a church family who has given her a place to belong.

A healthy church community is meant to be an extended family even for those with intact relationships with their family of origin. In fact, the New Testament writers use metaphors that point to this kind of shared, dependent life together: we are a body (1 Corinthians 12), a household (1 Timothy 3:15; 1 Peter 4:17), and a temple built of living stones (1 Corinthians 3:16–17; 1 Peter 2:4–5).

In 2020, 36.2 million Americans lived alone.[17] A local church can provide a sense of belonging and a network of care for those living far from family or who find themselves on their own. The stories of those who are alone merit attention.

In the 2004 movie *Shall We Dance?*, the character played by actress Susan Sarandon describes one purpose of marriage: "We need a witness to our lives. There's a billion people on the planet . . . I mean, what does any one life really mean? But in a marriage, you're promising to care about everything. The good things, the bad things, the terrible things, the mundane things . . . all of it, all of the time, every day. You're saying 'Your life will not go unnoticed, because I will notice it. Your life will not go un-witnessed, because I will be your witness.'"[18]

A functioning community of faith is a witness to the world precisely because members become witnesses to one another's lives as a reflection of the love God has for them.

We are who we are for a purpose

Jesus underscored to his disciples that commitment to him would shift or even sever the old group identities, even as he invited them into a new kind of family and faith (Mark 10:28–31). A sensitive translator of a family's past will endeavor to understand the way group identity is formed, and will recognize that racial, ethnic, and religious identity is developed by the relationships that members of the group have among themselves as well as their experiences with those outside the group. Translating the past means identifying how prejudices and assumptions inside and outside the group shaped the experiences of our forebears.

Interpreting that past in a spiritually healthy way means eschewing any sense of either superiority or self-loathing because of any of your unique, overlapping group identities. The apostle Paul wasn't erasing differences between groups when he wrote these words to his friends in Galatia. He was instead reminding them that all have an equal place in God's family because of their faith in the Lord Jesus:

> So in Christ Jesus you are all children of God through faith, for all of you who were baptized into Christ have clothed yourselves with Christ. There is neither Jew nor Gentile, neither slave nor free, nor is there male and female, for you are all one in Christ Jesus. If you belong to Christ, then you are Abraham's seed, and heirs according to the promise. (Galatians 3:26–29)

Our membership in God's family will change the way we relate to the world around us. Though group identities tend to create a sense of "us" versus "everyone else," belonging to God will connect us to others. John Donne's famous words are a reminder that isolating within a group's identity is not who we were created to be:

> No man is an island entire of itself; every man
> is a piece of the continent, a part of the main;
> if a clod be washed away by the sea, Europe
> is the less, as well as if a promontory were, as
> well as if a manor of thy friends or of thine
> own were; any man's death diminishes me,
> because I am involved in mankind.
> And therefore never send to know for whom
> the bell tolls; it tolls for thee.[19]

We can rightly begin to interpret the meaning of our membership within specific groups when we locate that understanding in the truth that our shared, interdependent humanity is a gift from God.

Reflect

1. As you consider your own growing-up years, how did your immediate family speak about their race? About other races?

2. What ethnic or cultural traditions are celebrated among your immediate or extended family?

3. Are you of the same faith tradition as your parents? Your grandparents? Why or why not?

NINE

From Generation to Generation

Seeing How Interpreting the Past Gives Meaning to Our Present and Helps Us Create an Informed, Faithful Legacy for the Future

ONCE UPON A TIME, there was no Wikipedia. When I was in elementary school during the 1960s, my family had a set of vintage World Book encyclopedias dating from the late 1940s. I was a voracious reader and worked my way through the entire set, from aardvark to zygote. I collected information the way other kids collected baseball cards. I was the rare teen who loved high school history class for the same reason I loved those old encyclopedias. The names and dates of those dusty history texts were more bits of delightful data to add to my disorganized mental hoard.

Data needs story to give it order, context, and meaning. Former high school social studies teacher Greg Milo makes this point well by asking readers to imagine how a dry, fact-focused history textbook might summarize the plot of the very first movie in the sprawling Star Wars saga:

> Like the Thirty Years' War in a World History course, the film would be only a small part of the overall course, and it might be in a chapter titled "The Galactic Empire" and look a little like this:
>
> > The Galactic Empire had increased its hold on a growing number of planets; however, the rebels continued to fight. In an effort to reign in the rebels, the Empire built a space station that could destroy a planet. In a show of power, the Empire destroyed the planet Alderaan, proving its strength.
> >
> > The Empire was planning on destroying more planets, which would certainly stall any rebel efforts, but during the Battle of Yavin, rebel pilots found a weakness and the space station was destroyed. This was a damaging blow to the Empire, and it was a huge boost to the rebel morale, but the Empire's growth was merely stalled.

There, that's the movie. That's what we ask students to learn about most wars in history. There are no specific players. There are no personal stories. There isn't much substance. And there's little doubt that the above version of Star Wars would not lead to a series of other movies, action figures, and kids' pajamas.[1]

Milo's history text treatment of the first installment of the sprawling film series makes the point that story calls for a different response from us than a stack of facts does. He writes, "We love stories that pull us in, stories that don't gloss over the excitement. We are drawn to stories that make us a part of it. That highlight the humanity. That require us to struggle with themes that we can relate to, like right and wrong or good and bad."

No story is more compelling than the one in which God has placed us. As we combine the streams of information flowing from various tributaries of our family's history into our lives, translating the past is not so much about documenting what happened once upon a time as it is about becoming more fully the people we were created to be.

History becomes our story

I once heard someone suggest in a tongue-in-cheek manner that we shouldn't attempt to teach history to people under age twenty-five, since younger people lack both the life experience and the adult-level reasoning skills to understand the relationships between people, places, and events.

To illustrate: The same year the Revolutionary War began in the American Colonies in 1776, did you know that a war was being fought in South America between Spain and Portugal, and another conflict took place between the Ottomans and the Persians in what is now known as Iran and Iraq? In 1776, the Bolshoi Ballet was founded in Moscow, Sir John Pringle published in London findings from Captain James Cook about how to prevent scurvy on long ocean voyages, Mozart's Serenade No. 7 premiered in Austria, and honor society Phi Beta Kappa originated at the College of William and Mary in Virginia. (See? I knew my propensity for gathering random bits of data would come in handy!)

None of these events happened in isolation. Each in some way was a response to what had occurred before 1776 and launched countless other events in the years to come. Every event changed for better or for worse the course of communities and nations—as well as individual lives. It is possible that at least one of these happenings may have touched your family's narrative in some way. In 1776, some of my husband's forebears living in the Thirteen Colonies joined the Revolutionary Army, and others remained loyal to the British—which offers some context to the decision one branch of the family made to head westward in the years immediately after the war. Mature translators will seek to make connections between the information they're gathering about their ancestors and what was happening in the world around the family in a particular place and time.

Crafting data into story is not unlike what weavers do as they shuttle a weft thread over and under the fixed, stationary warp threads in a loom. Historical events form a warp, and our family's story—complete with disparate data points, mysteries, and flesh-and-blood characters—is the weft that is woven in a one-of-a-kind pattern that transforms information into meaningful narrative. Writer Leslie Leyland Fields notes, "In our story . . . the words we braid and toss will coil and snarl between opposites, may tangle and resolve only to knot up again."[2] We can't untie every knot in our family's past, but we can gain insight that may untangle patterns and answer questions about our own lives while positioning us to offer hope and insight to those in the generations that follow us.

Rather than a loom, journaling may help you seek to weave data into story. You may be inspired to go a step further and turn your findings into a volume you can share with your extended family or your children—or even with a broader audience. Appendix A suggests resources that can help you get started if the process of interrogating the past has inspired you to write your story in order to share it with others.

However, the process of translating the past that I've described in the pages of this book is first and foremost an invitation to gain fluency so you can participate in ongoing dialogue between present and past. This is a discussion that will continue for the rest of your life. The Bible invites us continually into that conversation: "Remember the days of old; consider the generations long past. Ask your father and he will tell you, your elders, and they will explain to you" (Deuteronomy 32:7).

God will use the voices of our past in our present, even those belonging to deeply broken moral failures, to reveal the truth about who God is and who we are. *Shtisel*, a Hebrew- and Yiddish-language drama featuring an ultra-Orthodox Jewish family in Jerusalem, was a surprise hit for streaming service Netflix. In the remarkable final scene of the series, the aging patriarch of this complex brood cites an insight he gleaned from the writings of novelist Isaac Bashevis Singer as he ponders all the family members he's lost over his lifetime: "The dead don't go anywhere. They're all here. Each man is a cemetery. An actual cemetery, in which lie all our grandmothers and grandfathers, the father and mother, the wife, the child. Everyone is here all the time."[3]

When I was younger, I wished I could erase the painful chapters of my family's story and start my life afresh with a blank page. But I discovered the past didn't go away just because I wished it would. Curiosity has served me far better than avoidance ever has. As author Matthew Fox notes, "We learn about ourselves, our history and society by asking questions that expose the shadows in which we still live."[4]

Into the shadows, into the light

God's grace invites us to step into those shadows, because even the darkness is not dark to the one who is Light and Truth. Precious few of us inherit health, wealth, and a full slate of emotionally sound relatives. It is more likely that we'll find pain, shame, or sorrow hiding in the shadows of our family's history. The dialogue between past and present will break down for us if there are people in our past or present who we are struggling to forgive.

In some cases, forgiveness might seem impossible, perhaps because what a relative did was breathtakingly reprehensible, because you're not in contact with them at present, or because they've died. Some painful issues are best untangled with the interpretive help of a professional counselor, a seasoned pastor, or a spiritual director. Appendix B offers a few suggestions about how to find the help you may need.

But forgiveness isn't easy for any of us. In part, this is because forgiveness can be terribly misunderstood. Forgiveness does not mean trust is restored, the issue is forgotten, or that there's an automatic "and they all lived happily ever after" reconciliation. Forgiveness is our decision to release an offending person from the obligation to repay what the person has taken from us, whether that obligation is material, relational, or spiritual in nature. We can choose to forgive even if the person is no longer present in our lives.

Psychotherapist and pastor Nancy Collier describes forgiveness as "a decision to let the past be what it was, to leave it as is, imperfect and not what we wish it had been." She notes that unforgiveness keeps alive in us the impossible desire for a past different from the one that actually occurred, adding that forgiveness "takes the focus off of them; off waiting for and wanting them to be different, and moves towards ourselves, our own experience, our heart."[5]

Choosing to forgive can be an ongoing process for many of us. At the time Jesus lived, many rabbis taught that a person could be expected to forgive an offense a maximum of three times, following the pattern found in Amos 1:3–13.[6] Peter might have imagined he was far exceeding that figure when he asked Jesus whether he should forgive someone who sinned against him seven times, a number that represented God's perfection. Jesus responded with the stunning figure: not seven times, but seventy times seven (Matthew 18:21–22 GW). We are called to forgive again and again and again, just as God forgives each one of us.

The most profound image of forgiveness is found at the cross. Jesus' anguished words "Father, forgive them, for they do not know what they are doing" (Luke 23:34) hold living hope for us as we process the injustices in our story. Those who've wounded us can never know the extent of the pain they've caused. But the One crucified does, and in his perfect, overcoming love, he has promised to be with us as we navigate forgiveness for the 54th or 367th or 489th time.

Henri Nouwen writes, "Forgiveness is the name of love practiced among people who love poorly. The hard truth is that all people love poorly. We need to forgive and be forgiven every day, every hour increasingly. That is the great work of love among the fellowship of the weak that is the human family."[7] We have been loved poorly. And we love others imperfectly. A commitment to forgiveness allows us to understand our family story and ourselves from a posture of received mercy.

My own family forgiveness story includes that of a toxic church. When I was in my late twenties, I experienced a textbook case of spiritual abuse. Inadvertently, I stumbled a little too close to a secret about the pastor that had been closely guarded by my church leadership. In response, these trusted leaders branded me a problem in the congregation. A year of gossip, shunning, and emotional manipulation by these leaders followed. Because my relationship with my parents was strained because of my faith in Jesus, I counted on my church family's care and support. I was devastated by the betrayal by my leaders and the loss of community after we were asked to leave the church.

It was tempting to lean on what I'd learned in my family of origin—that unforgiveness was a virtue and a form of self-protection. But God used the truth of the Word and the persistence of a few faithful friends to prod me forward on what turned out to be a very long journey to forgive. During the next ten years, I heard from many others who'd left the church after receiving the same abusive treatment from leaders as I had. It was only when the pastor's wife left him that the truth at the root of the abuse was revealed: this popular pastor had for years lived a double life that included a porn addiction and an affair with a congregant. The church's governing elder team knew about his issues and had elected to cover it up because the church was growing numerically under this pastor's leadership. There was no joy or sense of vindication for me at the revelations. I grieved as I thought of the many, many lives that had been affected by the sin and cover-up, all to protect the false image of a "successful" church.

That experience helped me begin to learn the emotional and spiritual vocabulary of forgiveness. It taught me to remain vigilant about permitting bitterness to take root in my soul. It has been essential to my translation task.

Lewis Smedes was an influential presence in the area of forgiveness studies. He said, "Forgiving does not erase the bitter past. A healed memory is not a deleted memory. Instead, forgiving what we cannot forget creates a new way to remember. We change the memory of our past into a hope for our future."[8]

New ways to remember: The gifts of our story

When I first committed my life to Christ, I assumed that because my faith was different from that of my parents, my family story didn't much matter. After all, I was living for Jesus now! But that kind of narrow thinking kept me from fully embracing the good gifts God had given me through my forebears.

Faithful translators of the past will be as unflinching in our assessment of the goodness in our stories as we are in capturing the sorrows. Do you have ancestors who modeled self-sacrificing love? Expressed themselves with creativity? Faced adversity with courage?

When I first started writing during the 1980s and 1990s, I focused almost entirely on playwriting. There was no logical reason for this. No one in my immediate family was interested in theater, save for listening to the cast albums of popular Broadway musicals. I'd never even been in a school play. But when I was given an opportunity to create some scripts for a local children's radio show, I gave myself an immersion course in script-crafting by cleaning out the shelves on the topic at my local library, reading plays, and eavesdropping on conversations to study the rhythms of speech. I went on to write four full-length plays for the educational market and many skits for churches.

After my mom's funeral in 2007, a cousin who knew I was interested in my family story sent me some pictures of my mom's birth parents, Molly and George Klopman. Several of them featured young Molly with her Yiddish theater troupe in Poland before she immigrated to the United States in 1920. Some may mark this as merely an interesting coincidence. But I recognized the gift of creativity that Molly's life had deposited in my family story and gave thanks to God for it.[9]

Even the difficult parts of our family stories can be translated into our lives as gifts of resilience, empathy, and self-acceptance. The PBS show *Finding Your Roots* offers a compelling illustration of that possibility for all of us. Historian and professor Henry Louis Gates Jr. invites viewers along as he shares what he and his research team have uncovered about the genealogy and DNA connections of various celebrities who've agreed to be profiled. One especially memorable episode told the story of musician Pharrell Williams.[10] Gates read Williams an account from the sister of Williams's great-great-grandfather, a woman named Jane Arrington. Arrington's words were included in the Slave Narrative Project, a Works Project Administration effort that occurred during the height of the Great Depression and was designed to capture in their own words the experiences of formerly enslaved people before they all died.[11] Williams was so broken by her words about what his forebears had experienced that the crew had to stop filming and resume again another day after he took some time to process the information. He told Gates that this immersion into his family story had changed him. He expressed a desire to honor the courage and determination of his ancestors by the way he would use his voice in this world.

That exemplifies what translating the past can look like in our lives. While the past is our prologue, our present will be the prologue of those who come after us. Words attributed to the writer Philip Carr-Gomm say it well: "The songs of our ancestors are also the songs of our children."[12]

Singing a new old song

Songwriting requires a mastery of more than a language's vocabulary and grammar. Lyrics and poetry that have been translated from one language to another often sound clunky. Every language has its own rhythms, metaphors, and idioms. So too does every family story. And the only one who is equipped to interpret the past with the fluency of a native speaker into a song for the next generation is you. The song you as translator will sing to the next generations in your family will tell the story of your family's

Resilience
Curiosity
Honesty
Loss
Humility

Courage
Purpose
Failures
Secrets
Fears
Consequences
Trauma
Belonging
Disagreement
Faith
Hope
Love

We cannot dictate how we'll be remembered by our families and friends any more than the generations who came before us can tell us how they'd like to be remembered by us. But translating the past holds the promise of a more sure, solid sense of identity for us as we gain a more complete understanding of our story. The past may be prologue, but it is also a melody line that carries us into the future as we learn to sing the songs of our ancestors to our children.

The LORD is my inheritance and my cup.
You are the one who determines my destiny.
Your boundary lines mark out pleasant places for me.
Indeed, my inheritance is something beautiful.
(Psalm 16:5–6 GW)

Translator's Toolkit

*Have patience with everything that remains unsolved
in your heart. Try to love the questions themselves,
like locked rooms and like books written in a foreign
language. . . . At present you need to live the question.
Perhaps you will gradually, without even noticing it,
find yourself experiencing the answer, some distant day.*
—**RANIER MARIA RILKE**, Letters to a Young Poet[1]

MOST OF US are in the habit of googling our questions and receiving instant answers in response. Poet Ranier Maria Rilke's words from *Letters to a Young Poet* carry a great deal of wisdom for those of us seeking to translate our past. The questions that arise from translating our family stories rarely have quick or simple answers, but curiosity will keep us learning and growing—and can move us toward answers to those questions in the process.

Pastor and author Casey Tygrett notes that curiosity is an essential part of a maturing spiritual and emotional life: "Jesus took the disciples and introduced them to a life of engaging the questions. . . . As they grew, they also came to recognize they had a great deal more to explore. Curiosity didn't diminish in their time with Jesus; it took flight. That's what we're invited to."[2]

Choosing to live the questions can keep us prayerful and attentive as we learn to interpret the language spoken in each unique thread of our family story. The following section offers you space to begin your conversation with some of the questions raised in the pages of this book as well as a place to begin asking some of your own.

Chapter 1:
Message in a Bottle: Learning to Pay Attention to the Story the Past Is Telling Us

1. Is there anything holding you back from digging into your family story? In chapter 1, I named some possible reasons we may choose to forego exploring our past, including:

   - A family history marked by dysfunction
   - The impossibility of getting information about the past
   - Scattered, disconnected extended family
   - Complicated racial, ethnic, and religious factors
   - Fear of skeletons that may be lurking in the family closet

- Confusion about where to begin

- Disinterest

- Busyness

Resistance often holds an invitation to us. Is there a way you might be able to reframe your particular area or areas of resistance into the language of an invitation? For example, one way to reframe as an invitation the idea "It's impossible to get information about the past" might be "Learning about the past can be a learning experience as I discover how to get information about the past."

2. What questions about the past do you wish you could ask relatives who've died?

3. What questions do you have for God about your family story? Can you turn those questions into a prayer?

Chapter 2
The Original Family Tree: Anchoring Ourselves in a Larger Story as We Delve into Our Own Family History

1. As you reflect on the information in this chapter, was there anything that surprised you?

2. Is it difficult or easy for you to see yourself connected to the family tree described in Scripture? Why do you say so?

Chapter 3
Decoding the Double Helix: Deciphering the Language of Our DNA

1. Do you see physical resemblance between you and your parents, grandparents, or other relatives in your family of origin?

2. Are there any hereditary health issues or concerns in your medical history? How have those issues shown themselves in earlier generations in your family?

3. Do you recognize patterns of mental health struggle or addiction in your family's history? Was your family open about these issues?

4. Have you taken a consumer DNA test, such as those available from AncestryDNA, 23andMe, or Family-TreeDNA? If so, what were the results? Any surprises? Did the results lead you to any new connections with other branches of your family?

Chapter 4
The Unwanted "Gift" That Keeps Giving: Understanding How Trauma Can Encode Itself into Our Family History

1. Dr. Bessel van der Kolk cites these statistics from the Centers for Disease Control and Prevention: "One in five Americans was sexually molested as a child; one in four was beaten by a parent to the point of a mark being left on their body; and one in three couples engages in physical violence. A quarter of us grew up with alcoholic relatives, and one out of eight witnessed their mother being beaten or hit."[3] Do any of these statistics reflect your own experience? Do you know the stories of trauma that have happened to others in your family line? How has your family responded to and spoken about these experiences?

2. How have things like unexpected job loss, divorce, abandonment, financial failure, mental illness, premature death of a family member, or relocation affected the arc of your story?

3. As you consider the emerging science around the subject of epigenetic trauma, are there events from previous generations that may have contributed to changed physical or emotional responses in subsequent generations in your family?

Chapter 5
Patterns and Promises: Identifying the Consequences of Our Forebears' Decisions

1. Have you seen repeating destructive patterns of upheaval or chaos at work from generation to generation in your family? If so, how did they play out?

2. Are there promises you made to yourself when you were younger that have had a negative impact on the way you've lived your life? What was the reason for those vows? What did those events teach you about God, other people, and yourself? Is there a lie at the foundation of that vow in your life? What truth might supplant that lie?

Chapter 6
Filling In the Blanks: Listening to the Mysteries in Our Family Narrative

1. Can you name the gaps, silences, and mysteries in your family's story? What questions do you have about what filled those negative spaces?

2. How long has your immediate family lived in its current location? What about your extended family? Can you trace the movements of your forebears through previous generations? Where did they live? What caused them to move? Who or what did they leave behind?

Chapter 7
For This Child I Prayed: Discovering the Blessings and Challenges of Adoption in a Family's Story

1. Has adoption been a part of your family history? Has it been a story of redemption, an experience filled with challenge, or a mix of both?

2. In this chapter, I described the seven core lifelong issues of adoption:

   Loss
   Rejection
   Shame and guilt
   Grief
   Identity
   Intimacy
   Mastery and control

   If adoption is part of your story, in what ways have you seen these issues present themselves among various members of the adoption constellation?

3. Is it easy or painful to consider what it might look like at this point in your life to honor your birth parents? Your adoptive parents? Other key caregivers in your life?

Chapter 8
Who Are My People? Discerning How Race, Ethnicity, and Religion Shaped the Experience and Identity of Our Ancestors

1. Can you describe your race or races? What has been your experience as a member of that community (or communities) in this world? What was the experience of your forebears? Was there a history of bias or prejudice against their racial group or groups? Have there been things in recent years that have challenged your understanding as a member of that group or those groups?

2. What ethnic or cultural traditions are celebrated among your immediate or extended family? How important are those ethnic or cultural origins in your family? As family members married outside of that ethnic tradition in the past, how did couples navigate the differences?

3. Are you of the same faith tradition as those in earlier generations of your family? Why or why not?

4. If you have been part of a church as an adult, how has the experience contributed to your understanding of who you are as a person? As a follower of Christ?

Chapter 9
From Generation to Generation: Seeing How Interpreting the Past Gives Meaning to Our Present and Helps Us Create an Informed, Faithful Legacy for the Future

1. Write a letter to your great-great-grandchild or to someone who might be living in the future four generations hence. What do you want them to know about your story? About the world in which you're living?

2. As you reflect on what you know of your family story, what themes most stand out to you? How have those themes played themselves out in your life?

3. Are there people in your family story, living or dead, whom you struggle to forgive? What might it look like to develop a new way to remember those relationships?

4. As you reflect on your family story, what is most beautiful to you about it? What might be in the song God has given you to sing to the next generation in your family, church, and community? Even if it is only one or two words today, offer those words to God in a prayer, asking for help as you continue in the ongoing mission to translate your past.

Additional Resources

NOT EVERY BOOK or website listed below is written for a Christian audience, but each offers information that may be of help for those looking to dig deeper into various aspects of their family stories.

Creating a family tree

- "Family Tree Maker" from Canva (https://www.canva .com/graphs/family-trees/)—This free online design tool offers some easy-to-use options.

- FamilySearch.com—Another free option to start designing your own family tree. This site, run by the Church of Jesus Christ of Latter-day Saints (commonly known as the Mormon Church), offers genealogical researchers access to their massive database of information.

- "Family Tree Templates for Non-traditional Families" from Family Tree Templates (https://www.familytreetemplates .net/category/nontraditional)—This site has some helpful choices for those looking to create a family tree for stepfamilies, adoptive families, and other nontraditional families.

- Ancestry.com, FamilyTree.com—These consumer DNA testing sites offer online tools for those who wish to build a family tree connected with the results of their genetic tests, and also offer memberships for those searching the providers' databases for birth, immigration, marriage, death records, and more as they pull together their family's history.

- There are also several paid software options. I can't recommend one over another, but if you're looking to catalog lots of data, including pictures, records, and letters, comparing the features and reviews of dedicated genealogy software tools might be your best bet.

Capturing family history

- "Conducting Oral Histories with Family Members" from the UCLA Library (https://www.library.ucla.edu/location/library-special-collections/location/center-oral-history-research/resources/conducting-oral-histories-family-members)—A comprehensive overview of a formal process for gathering and transcribing stories from family members.

- "Interviewing Questions and Prompts for Family History Interviews" from *Family Tree Magazine* (https://www.familytreemagazine.com/storytelling/interviewing/interview-questions/)—Questions you can use to spark stories from relatives. (Make sure to have a recording device handy and a plan to transcribe the information when you start asking questions!)

- "Great Questions" from StoryCorps (https://storycorps.org/participate/great-questions/)—Wonderful informal prompts to stir memories and spark conversation with family.

- "The 'Do You Know?' 20 Questions about Family Stories" on *Psychology Today* (https://www. psychologytoday.com/us/blog/the-stories-our-lives/201611/the-do-you-know-20-questions-about-family-stories)—A complete list of the "Do You Know?" tool used by researchers Robyn Fivush and Marshall Duke referenced in chapter 1.

Additional visual tools you can use to help document your family story

- Timelines—Create a timeline of key dates (marriages, births, deaths, relocations, business launches) in your family's history. Add dates of key world or cultural events, such as World War II or the moon landing.

- Photo albums—It is amazing how quickly names and dates disappear from memory when it comes to old albums. If possible, enlist the assistance of an older relative to help add this data where possible.

- Calendars—Create a list of family members' birth dates, wedding anniversaries, and dates of deaths.

- Cultural family trees—Create a family tree that traces the ethnic and cultural origins of each generation of the family, noting where individuals were born and how they expressed their cultural identities.

- Family treasures—Many have on hand at least a few treasured family heirlooms like an antique quilt or a set of candlesticks. Who currently possesses these items, and where are they housed? What is the origin of each item? Documenting the item's history can help the item's caretakers in the next generation.

The Bible's genealogies and possible timelines for recorded events

- "Bible Family Tree" (biblefamilytree.info/)—A visual map of all the names in the Bible.

- "Bible Tree Chart" from ACTS Cambridge (http://www .actscambridge.org/assets/images/bible_genealogy_a1_ chart.pdf)—A chart of the Bible's genealogy.

- "Jesus and Genealogies" (https://bibleproject.com/blog/ jesus-genealogies/)—A helpful explainer about the New Testament genealogies of Jesus.

- *Jesus' Family Tree: Seeing God's Faithfulness in the Genealogy of Christ* (Peabody, MA: Rose Publishing, 2014).

- *Essential Guide to the Genealogy of Jesus* (Peabody, MA: Rose Publishing, 2021).

- Linda Finlayson, *God's Bible Timeline: The Big Book of Biblical History* (Fearn, UK: CF4Kids, 2020). This book is aimed at a children's audience, but can help grownups too.

Genetics

- Biologos.org—BioLogos is a solid general resource for searchable science information from a thoughtful faith perspective.

- CBHD.org—The Center for Bioethics and Human Dignity is an academic think tank that addresses moral and ethical questions in science and medicine.

- Francis S. Collins, *The Language of God: A Scientist Presents Evidence for Belief* (Washington, DC: Free Press, 2007). Collins, a Christian, was the head of the Human Genome Project, is a former president of BioLogos, and was recently director of the National Institutes for Health. This book offers a look at the relationship between science and faith.

- Scot McKnight and Dennis Venema, *Adam and the Genome: Reading Scripture after Genetic Science* (Ada, MI: Brazos, 2017). A scientist and a theologian pair up to talk about genetics, evolution, and the historical Adam.

- G. K. Chesterton, *Eugenics and Other Evils* (London: Cassell, 1922), now available in the public domain via Kindle. It is chilling to read the prophetic words written by this beloved thinker and cultural critic while the idea of eugenics was gaining traction in the West and before it was embraced by Nazi Germany.

Trauma

- Bessel van der Kolk, *The Body Keeps the Score: Brain, Mind, and Body in the Healing of Trauma* (New York: Viking, 2014). This essential text has given an entire generation tools to understand the effect of trauma on our bodies and minds.

- Mark Wolynn, *It Didn't Start with You: How Inherited Family Trauma Shapes Who We Are and How to End The*

Cycle (New York: Penguin, 2016). Wolynn has identified a variety of ways unresolved family issues are transmitted from generation to generation.

- Sheila Wise Rowe, *Healing Racial Trauma: The Road to Resilience* (Westmont, IL: InterVarsity Press, 2020). Wise Rowe focuses on racial trauma in this book, and her insight offers hope and pathways toward healing that touch on other kinds of trauma as well.

- Curt Thompson, *Anatomy of the Soul: Surprising Connections between Neuroscience and Spiritual Practices That Can Transform Your Life and Relationships* (Carol Stream, IL: 2010). This helpful text links science-based insight with life-giving spiritual practices.

- Biobeats, "How Unprocessed Trauma Is Stored In The Body," Medium, January 21, 2020, https://medium.com/@biobeats/how-unprocessed-trauma-is-stored-in-the-body-10222a76cbad. This short piece describes how our bodies warehouse trauma.

- Martha Henriques, "Can The Legacy of Trauma Be Passed Down The Generations?," BBC, March 26, 2019, https://www.bbc.com/future/article/20190326-what-is-epigenetics. A long read that offers a good overview of the emerging science of epigenetics.

- "The Legacy of Trauma: Can Experiences Leave a Biological Imprint?" NPR, February 25, 2021, https://www.npr.org/transcripts/947232031. A recording and transcript of a National Public Radio conversation about epigenetics.

The question of evil

- C. S. Lewis, *The Problem of Pain* (New York: Harper Collins, 2012). The always thought-provoking Lewis avoids easy answers to the question of why a good God permits suffering in this world.

- N. T. Wright, *Evil and the Justice of God* (Westmont, IL: InterVarsity Press, 2007). Wright asks readers to consider the implications of justice as they wrestle with the issue of evil.

- Kate Bowler, *Everything Happens for a Reason: And Other Lies I've Loved* (New York: Random House, 2018). Theologian Bowler received a life-altering diagnosis at a young age. This memoir invites readers into her struggle to understand the incomprehensible.

Generational consequences and vows

- Chad Ashby, "Recognizing 'The Sins of Our Fathers' Means Admitting We're Their Children," *Christianity Today*, October 29, 2020, https://www.christianitytoday.com/ct/2020/october-web-only/reckoning-with-original-sin-race-injustice.html. A balanced take on the subject of generational sin.

- Ronald T. Hyman, "Four Acts of Vowing in The Bible," JewishBible, https://jbqnew.jewishbible.org/assets/Uploads/374/374_vowsfinal.pdf. A helpful exploration of vows in the Old Testament.

- John Paul II Healing Center, "Healing the Whole Person," Franklin Hardin Catholic, accessed October 26, 2021, franklinhardincatholic.org/wp-content/uploads/Seven

-Deadly-Wounds.pdf. This brief summary was created by a Catholic healing center. It links the core kinds of vows we make to the seven deadly sins.

- Gary Wetzel, "All the Blessings and Benedictions in the Bible," Worshipping with God's Word, last modified May 10, 2021, https://worshippingwithgodsword.com/all-the-benedictions-in-the-bible. A comprehensive list of all the verses in the Bible that include blessings.

The gaps in our family narrative

- "8 Tips to Find Your Family Tree," *National Geographic*, December 8, 2017, https://www.nationalgeographic.com/travel/article/genealogy-heritage-travel-roots-tips. A helpful overview about how to dig into gaps and questions in your genealogical research.

- Sophie Kay, "Negative Space: Making Your Genealogy Gaps Work For You (and Your Family Tree)," *The Parchment Rustler* (blog), September 30, 2020, https://parchmentrustler.com/family-history/negative-space. This piece offers some perspective on those gaps and questions in your family story.

- Sheri McGregor, *Done with the Crying: Help and Meaning for Mothers of Estranged Adult Children* (San Marcos, CA: Sowing Creek Press, 2016). The focus of this book is on helping parents process estrangement from their adult children.

Adoption

- "Adoption History in Brief," University of Oregon, February 24, 2012, https://pages.uoregon.edu/adoption/topics/adoptionhistbrief.htm. An overview of adoption history.

- Sharon Kaplan Roszia and Allison Davis Maxon, "Seven Core Issues in Adoption and Permanency," *Adoptalk*, no. 2 (August 15, 2019), https://www.nacac.org/resource/seven-core-issues-in-adoption-and-permanency. An excellent introduction to the seven core issues in adoption.

- Mary Rentschler, "Constellations for Adoption," Constellations Group, last modified August 19, 2021, https://www.theconstellationsgroup.com/articles/constellations-for-adoption.html. A helpful discussion about the members of the adoption constellation.

- Brenda McCreight, "Attachment Disorder and the Adoptive Family," Dave Thomas Foundation, March 2015, https://davethomasfoundation.org/wp-content/uploads/2015/03/Attachment-pamphlet.pdf. An in-depth look at the topic of attachment in foster and adopted children.

- Karyn B. Purvis, David R. Cross, and Wendy Lyons Sunshine, *The Connected Child: Bring Hope and Healing to Your Adopted Child* (New York: McGraw-Hill, 2007). This handbook for parents can help those seeking to learn more about attachment topics.

- Jennifer Grant, *Love You More: The Divine Surprise of Adopting My Daughter* (Nashville: Thomas Nelson, 2011). A wise and lovely memoir about the international adoption process.

Racial and cultural identity

- Christian Smith and Michael O. Emerson, *Divided by Faith: Evangelical Religion and the Problem of Race in America* (Oxford University Press, 2001). Though now more than two decades old, this book contains a still-relevant look at the relationship between race and religion in America.

- Jemar Tisby, *The Color of Compromise: The Truth about the American Church's Complicity in Racism* (Zondervan, 2020). An essential discussion about the church and racism.

- Rob Muthiah et al., *Lamenting Racism* video series and study guides (Harrisonburg, VA: Herald Press, 2021). A useful tool for groups who want to contemplate together the effects of racism.

- Patrice Gopo, *All the Colors We Will See: Reflections on Barriers, Brokenness, and Finding Our Way* (Nashville, Thomas Nelson, 2018). This title touches on issues of immigration and race.

- Isabel Wilkerson, *Caste: The Origins of Our Discontents* (New York: Random House, 2020). Offers a different lens through which to understand issues of race and culture.

- Jenny McGill, *Religious Identity and Cultural Negotiation: Toward a Theology of Christian Identity in Migration* (Eugene, OR: Pickwick Publications, 2016). This academic book offers insight into the development of religious and cultural identity.

Forgiveness

- Lewis B. Smedes, *The Art of Forgiving: When You Need to Forgive and Don't Know How* (New York: Ballantine/ Random House, 1996). This book, along with all Smedes's other writing, offers help and profound insight into the process of forgiveness.

- Viktor Frankl, *Man's Search for Meaning* (Boston: Beacon Press, 2006). This classic work by concentration camp survivor and therapist Frankl talks about building a life despite injustice and tragedy.

- Donald B. Kraybill, Steven M. Nolt, David L. Weaver-Zercher, *Amish Grace: How Forgiveness Transcended Tragedy* (San Francisco: Jossey-Bass, 2010). The authors explore how the Amish community expressed forgiveness in the wake of the 2006 West Nickel Mines School mass shooting.

- Leslie Leyland Fields and Dr. Jill Hubbard, *Forgiving Our Fathers and Mothers: Finding Freedom From Hurt and Hate* (Carol Stream, IL: Tyndale, 2014). This book offers rich insight into forgiving the unforgivable.

- Pete Scazzero, *Emotionally-Healthy Discipleship: Moving from Shallow Christianity to Deep Transformation* (Grand Rapids: Zondervan, 2021). Scazzero's focus is on integration and growth, and forgiveness is a key part of that emphasis.

Finding a counselor

- One place to begin finding a counselor is by asking for recommendations from people you know and trust: family, friends, and your church. Your insurance company can be of assistance not only with helping you understand your benefits but also by providing lists of counselors covered under your plan.

- "How Do I Find a Good Therapist?," APA, July 2017, https://www.apa.org/ptsd-guideline/patients-and-families/finding-good-therapist. The American Psychological Association offers some practical tips and questions to consider as you're looking for a counselor.

- "Finding a Christian Therapist" from *Psychology Today* (https://www.psychologytoday.com/us/therapists/christian)—While a good counselor will respect your faith even if they don't share it, many Christians prefer to seek a licensed counselor who identifies as a believer. This site offers a searchable listing of some Christian counselors in every state.

- OpenPathCollective.org—This site offers searchable options as well.

Finding a spiritual director

- A spiritual director is not a professional counselor or a life coach, but a person committed to journey with you to discern how God is at work in your life. The Diocese of St. Albans website explains, "Spiritual directors are people of prayer and integrity, who are self-aware and are particularly conscious of their own frailty and need of God. They will be aware of the riches of spiritual wisdom to be found in Scripture and in our Christian heritage. Their love for God and their experience of the love of God will enhance their care for others and enrich their listening and their empathy."[1]

- There is a long tradition of spiritual direction in Catholicism, and a growing attention to this discipline in many other Protestant streams of the church as well. You don't necessarily need to come from the same denominational tradition as that of your spiritual director. That said, your pastor or another trusted church leader may be able to suggest a spiritual director. There are a variety of training organizations for spiritual directors out there, and these can also point you toward someone who might be a good fit, including

  ○ Network of Evangelical Spiritual Directors (https://www.networkofevangelicalspiritualdirectors.com)

  ○ The Transforming Center (https://transformingcenter .org/spiritual-direction-4/)

Writing family stories

- Diane Haddad, "9 Tips for Getting Started Writing Your Family History," *Family Tree Magazine*, last modified April 6, 2021, https://www.familytreemagazine.com/storytelling/tips-getting-started-writing-family-history/. Helpful tips for starting to write your family history.

- Leslie Leyland Fields, *Your Story Matters: Finding, Writing, and Living the Truth of Your Life* (Colorado Springs: NavPress, 2020). This step-by-step guide will help you discover how to tell your story in a meaningful way.

- "Everything Memoir," *Susy Flory* (blog), January 31, 2020, http://www.susyflory.com/blog). *New York Times* bestselling author Susy Flory offers workshops and resources for those looking to write their story.

Acknowledgments

TO EACH PERSON who trusted me with their stories, thank you for inviting me to stand on holy ground with you. I am humbled by your willingness to share your experiences with such grace and courage. I pray I've honored you with my words.

I'm grateful for the networks of support that have carried me during the writing process, the care of insightful friends in the Pelican Project, and the members of Ink Creative Collective, Susy Flory, Jennifer Grant, and Marlena Graves. If a good word at the right time is akin to golden apples set in silver, as Proverbs 25:11 says it is, each one of you gave me a platinum apple at a time when I needed it most.

I'm deeply appreciative for the support of pals Anita Lustrea and Melinda Schmidt. I listened to your wisdom for years when you co-hosted a radio show that played a significant role in my spiritual formation, and now I'm grateful to call you friends in real life. A couple of pivotal conversations with Judi Sandiford helped guide my research in the early stages of writing. Christy Glick's keen insights guided me as I revised my work. I thank God continually for the love and prayer support of my prayer partner of more than two decades, Meg Kausalik. God has used our rabbit-trail conversations and ongoing prayer to give me insight into key elements of my past. Spiritual director Janet Davis has been both advocate and encourager. Her belief in this project has meant the world to me. And I am grateful for the support of my cemetery-walking sister in faith, Margaret Wheeler. This entire book is a memorial stone.

My agent, Steve Laube, gave me the title for this book and lots of encouragement as I was incubating this project. I'm delighted to be working with acquisitions editor Laura Leonard after we first connected more than a decade ago writing for the Her.meneutics blog at *Christianity Today*. The team at Herald Press has been warm and supportive every step of the way. Thank you!

Though I never had an opportunity to meet my maternal grandmother, Molly Klopman, her story has shaped my life in profound ways. I am exceedingly grateful for each forebear on my family tree, as well as for the lives of those who will sing our family song after I'm gone—my three children, two grandsons, and the rest of those in our family circle. And to Bill, who has not only endured the strange life that comes from being married to a writer but celebrates it—and loves me faithfully and well.

Writing acknowledgments is a way of giving thanks to the Giver of these remarkable gifts. Heavenly Father, it took me a long time to recognize just how rich my family story is. Thank you for the gift of your Son, who, through the power of your Spirit, continues to teach me to sing a new song.

Notes

Introduction

1 William Shakespeare, *The Tempest*, ed. Charles W. Eliot (New York: P.F. Collier, 1909–14; Bartleby.com, 2001), 2.1.248–49.

2 Bijay Kumar Das, *A Handbook of Translation Studies* (Delhi: Atlantic Publishers, 2005), 58.

Chapter 1

1 Gregory Rodriguez, "How Genealogy Became Almost as Popular as Porn," *Time*, May 30, 2014, https://time.com/133811/how-genealogy-became-almost-as-popular-as-porn/. Note: Black women weren't admitted into the Daughters of the American Revolution until the same year that *Roots* premiered—1977. Deepti Hajela, "'Daughters' Welcomes 1st Black Woman to National Board," AP News, June 29, 2019, https://apnews.com/8405c614f6df4ecfaac22c5e2e757736.

2 Juliana Szucs, "How 1970s 'Roots' Inspired a Generation of Family History Researchers," Ancestry, May 27, 2016, https://blogs.ancestry.com/ancestry/2016/05/27/how-1970s-roots-inspired-a-generation-of-family-history-researchers/.

3 *The Complete Works of Ralph Waldo Emerson*, vol. 8, *Letters and Social Aims* (Boston: Houghton, Mifflin, 1875), 176.

4 "How to Find the Holy Grail of Chinese Genealogy" Legacy Tree Genealogists, last modified November 26, 2018, https://www.legacytree.com/blog/chinese-genealogy-holy-grail. *Patrilineal* refers to the relationship to the father, traced through the father's family line.

5 "How to Find the Holy Grail."

6 "Oral Genealogies," Family Search, last modified August 6, 2021, https://www.familysearch.org/wiki/en/Oral_Genealogies.

7 Robyn Fivush, "Why We Need Stories More Than Ever," *Psychology Today*, July 31, 2020, https://www.psychologytoday.com/us/blog/the-stories-our-lives/202007/why-we-need-stories-more-ever.

8 Cheryl Proska, "The Importance and Benefits of Family Storytelling," *Friends Life Care* (blog), July 5, 2017, https://www.friendslifecare.org/the-importance-benefits-of-family-storytelling/.

9 Robyn Fivush, "The 'Do You Know?' 20 Questions about Family Stories," *Psychology Today*, November 19, 2016, https://www.psychologytoday.com/us/blog/the-stories-our-lives/201611/the-do-you-know-20-questions-about-family-stories.

10 Mary W. Quigley, "Here Is Why You Should Share Family Stories," *AARP Blogs*, August 4, 2014, https://blog.aarp.org/parenting-part-2/here-is-why-you-should-share-family-stories.

11 I explore this process at length in my book *If Only: Letting Go of Regret* (Kansas City, MO: Beacon Hill, 2014).

Chapter 2

1 John Millam, "The Genesis Genealogies," revised June 2010, https://s3.amazonaws.com/reasonstobelieve/files/articles/The-Genesis-Genealogies.pdf.

2 When ancient authors used numbers, they were concerned with conveying sacred meaning. The number seventy is made up of the multiplier of two essential numbers: seven, which represents perfection and reflects God's perfect creation, and ten, which points at the completeness of Ten Commandments, and by extension, the entire Law. It is a number that is used

throughout Scripture to highlight perfect spiritual order, as in the appointment of seventy elders by Moses (Numbers 11:16), as well as judgment, as in the captivity in Babylon (Jeremiah 29:10). This first use of the number seventy in Genesis 10 points to the goodness and perfection of God's work in the post-flood world. "Meaning of Numbers in the Bible," Bible Study, last modified August 9, 2021, https://www.biblestudy .org/bibleref/meaning-of-numbers-in-bible/70.html.

3 Hagar became a part of Abram's traveling clan after his sojourn in Egypt. See Genesis 12:10.

4 Ishmael's immediate descendants are named in the family tree mentioned in Genesis 25:12–18.

5 Abraham sought a wife for his child of promise not from among people local to him in his new home in Canaan, but from among his family's people in Ur (Genesis 24).

6 Exodus 12:37 states that there were six hundred thousand adult men in this company. The figure is meant to remind us that Abraham's descendants were becoming as numerous as the stars in the sky, even under generations of oppressive conditions in Egypt.

7 We'll look more closely at David's troubled relationship with a couple of his sons in chapter 6.

8 The books of Daniel and Esther record events that occurred during the Babylonian captivity and illustrate the commitment to God alone that emerged during this time of discipline, loss, and sorrow among the people of Judah.

9 Generations earlier, in the Sinai Desert, God had expressly forbidden his people to intermarry people from surrounding nations (Deuteronomy 7:1–11). Some of those returning from Babylon had brought along their foreign wives. These wives and their children would not be able to serve the gods of Babylon in a revived Judah. Ezra 10 contains a list of the names of those who agreed to dissolve these unions in order to return to God.

10 One notable exception was the Maccabean revolt in 167 BC. This event is remembered and celebrated during the Jewish holiday of Hanukkah each year.

11 "Why Do Matthew and Luke's Genealogies Contradict One Another?," Bible.org, accessed March 17, 2021, https://bible.org/question/why-do-matthew-and-lukes-genealogies-contradict-one-another.

Chapter 3

1 "Has the Consumer DNA Test Boom Gone Bust?," Advisory, February 20, 2020, https://www.advisory.com/en/daily-briefing/2020/02/20/dna-tests. FamilyTree DNA was the first direct-to-consumer test. It came to market in 2000.

2 For those seeking DNA connections with those who've taken different tests, GEDmatch.com aggregates data from across many platforms for those who upload their data to the site.

3 Sam Kean, "Unraveling the Genetic Code That Makes Us Human," NPR, June 23, 2012, https://www.npr.org/2012/07/23/157231248/unraveling-the-genetic-code-that-makes-us-human.

4 Sam Kean, *The Violinist's Thumb: And Other Lost Tales of Love, War, and Genius, as Written by Our Genetic Code* (New York: Little, Brown, 2013), introduction.

5 Since my diagnosis in 2016, I've received infusions of a plasma-based immunoglobulin treatment that replaces some, but not all, of what my body does not manufacture on its own.

6 According to the National Organization for Rare Disorders, "Tay-Sachs disease occurs with greater frequency among Jewish people of Ashkenazi descent, i.e. those of Eastern or Central European descent. Approximately one in 30 Ashkenazi Jewish people carries the altered gene for Tay-Sachs disease. In addition, one in 300 individuals of non-Ashkenazi Jewish heritage is a carrier." Rare Disease Database, s.v. "Tay Sachs Disease," accessed May 18, 2021, https://rarediseases.org/rare-diseases/tay-sachs-disease/.

7 The names and some identifying details of this story have been changed at the request of the family.

8 Libby Copeland, "Genetic Testing Is Changing Our Understanding of Who Fathers Are," *Washington Post*, June 21, 2021, https://www.washingtonpost.com/outlook/dna-testing-fathers/

2021/06/17/7f607c54-ce20-11eb-8cd2-4e95230cfac2_story
.html.

9 Dani Shapiro, *Inheritance: A Memoir of Genealogy, Paternity,
and Love* (New York: Anchor Books, 2019), 35.

10 Quoted in Mark Silk, "Did John Adams Out Thomas Jefferson
and Sally Hemings?," *Smithsonian*, November 2016, https://
www.smithsonianmag.com/history/john-adams-out-thomas
-jefferson-sally-hemings-180960789/. Capitalization and italics
in the original.

11 "Monticello Affirms Thomas Jefferson Fathered Children with
Sally Hemings," Monticello, accessed March 28, 2021, https://
www.monticello.org/thomas-jefferson/jefferson-slavery/thomas
-jefferson-and-sally-hemings-a-brief-account/monticello
-affirms-thomas-jefferson-fathered-children-with-sally
-hemings/. Note: There are dissenting voices who dispute these
findings: "Jefferson's Blood: Is It True?," *Frontline*, accessed
March 28, 2021, https://www.pbs.org/wgbh/pages/frontline/
shows/jefferson/true/.

12 Britni Danielle, "Sally Hemings Wasn't Thomas Jefferson's
Mistress. She Was His Property," *Washington Post*, July 6, 2017,
https://www.washingtonpost.com/outlook/sally-hemings
-wasnt-thomas-jeffersons-mistress-she-was-his-property/2017/
07/06/db5844d4-625d-11e7-8adc-fea80e32bf47_story.html.

13 "Thomas Jefferson and Sally Hemings: A Brief Account," Monticello, accessed March 28, 2021, https://www.monticello.org/
thomas-jefferson/jefferson-slavery/thomas-jefferson-and-sally
-hemings-a-brief-account/.

14 Michael White, "How Slavery Changed the DNA of African
Americans," *Pacific Standard*, last modified December 20, 2017,
https://psmag.com/news/how-slavery-changed-the-dna-of
-african-americans.

15 Frank Harris III, "To the White Members of My Family Tree,"
Hartford Courant, September 5, 2019, https://www.courant
.com/opinion/op-ed/hc-op-frank-harris-whites-family-tree
-0905-20190905-phdvsqnl6fcdhjf7eb4k7vmpke-story.html;
study referenced in Harris' piece is Katarzyna Bryc et al., "The
Genetic Ancestry of African Americans, Latinos, and European

Americans across the United States," *American Journal of Human Genetics* 96, no. 1 (January 8, 2015): 37–53, https://doi.org/10.1016/j.ajhg.2014.11.010.

16 Eli Baden-Lazar, "I'm 20. I Have 32 Half Siblings. This Is My Family Portrait," *New York Times*, June 26, 2019, https://www.nytimes.com/interactive/2019/06/26/magazine/sperm-donor-siblings.html.

17 J. Budziszewski, *What We Can't Not Know: A Guide* (San Francisco: Ignatius Press, 2011), 75.

18 Joel Eissenberg, "Discoveries in DNA: What's New Since You Went to High School?," Saint Louis University, August 2016, https://www.slu.edu/news/2016/august/Eissenberg-genetics-essay.php.

19 Francis Galton, *Hereditary Genius: An Inquiry into Its Laws and Consequences*, reprint ed. (London: Macmillan, 1892), 1. First published 1869.

20 "Eugenics Records Office (ERO)," Eugenics Archive, last modified December 6, 2011, http://www.eugenicsarchive.org/html/eugenics/static/themes/20.html.

21 G. K. Chesterton, *Eugenics and Other Evils* (London: Cassel and Company, 1922), 19. Italics in the original.

22 Lisa Ko, "Unwanted Sterilization and Eugenics Programs in the United States," *Beyond the Films*, January 29, 2016, https://www.pbs.org/independentlens/blog/unwanted-sterilization-and-eugenics-programs-in-the-united-states/.

23 "The Supreme Court Ruling That Led To 70,000 Forced Sterilizations," *Fresh Air*, March 7, 2016, https://www.npr.org/sections/health-shots/2016/03/07/469478098/the-supreme-court-ruling-that-led-to-70-000-forced-sterilizations.

24 Tom Head, "Forced Sterilization in the United States," ThoughtCo, last modified August 9, 2021, https://www.thoughtco.com/forced-sterilization-in-united-states-721308.

25 Janelli Vallin, "California Needs to Repair the Damage from Its History of Systematic Sterilizations," CalMatters, January 7, 2021, https://calmatters.org/commentary/my-turn/2021/01/california-needs-to-repair-the-damage-from-its-history-of

-systematic-sterilizations/.

26 United States Holocaust Memorial Museum, "Nazi Racism: An Overview," Holocaust Encyclopedia, accessed March 30, 2021, https://encyclopedia.ushmm.org/content/en/article/nazi -racism-an-overview.

27 "The Biological State: Nazi Racial Hygiene, 1933–1939," Holocaust Encyclopedia, accessed March 30, 2021, https:// encyclopedia.ushmm.org/content/en/article/the-biological -state-nazi-racial-hygiene-1933-1939.

28 Francis Collins, *The Language of God: A Scientist Presents Evidence for Belief* (New York: Free Press, 2006), 123–24.

Chapter 4

1 The names and some identifying details of this story have been changed.

2 "Trauma," American Psychological Association, accessed April 17, 2021, https://www.apa.org/topics/trauma.

3 Bessel van der Kolk, *The Body Keeps the Score: Brain, Mind, and Body in the Healing of Trauma* (New York: Penguin Books, 2014), 1.

4 Marissa Moore, "Types of PTSD," PsychCentral, last modified May 23, 2021, https://psychcentral.com/lib/types-of-ptsd.

5 Van der Kolk, *Body Keeps the Score*, 20–21.

6 "Patrick McKenna" is a fictitious character.

7 Mark Wolynn, *It Didn't Start with You: How Inherited Family Trauma Shapes Who We Are and How To End The Cycle* (New York: Penguin, 2016), 22–23.

8 Wolynn, 157.

9 Laura Elnitski, "Epigenetics," National Human Genome Research Institute, accessed April 17, 2021, https://www.genome .gov/genetics-glossary/Epigenetics.

10 Quoted in Siddhartha Mukherjee, "Same but Different: How Epigenetics Can Blur the Line between Nature and Nurture," *New Yorker*, April 25, 2016, https://www.newyorker.com/ magazine/2016/05/02/breakthroughs-in-epigenetics.

11 Lara Marks, "Epigenetics," What Is Biotechnology, June 2017, https://www.whatisbiotechnology.org/index.php/science/summary/epigenetics/.

12 Quoted in Mukherjee, "Same but Different."

13 Rae Ellen Bichell, "Scientists Start to Tease Out the Subtler Ways Racism Hurts Health," *Weekend Edition Saturday*, November 11, 2017, https://www.npr.org/sections/health-shots/2017/11/11/562623815/scientists-start-to-tease-out-the-subtler-ways-racism-hurts-health.

14 Vickie M. Mays, Susan D. Cochran, and Namdi W. Barnes, "Race, Race-Based Discrimination, and Health Outcomes among African Americans," *Annual Review of Psychology* 58 (January 2007): 201–25, https://dx.doi.org/10.1146/annurev.psych.57.102904.190212.

15 Myra Goodman, "My Holocaust Survivor Parents Never Talked about It—and Their Silence Didn't Protect Me," Salon, January 27, 2020, https://www.salon.com/2020/01/27/my-holocaust-survivor-parents-never-talked-about-it--and-their-silence-didnt-protect-me/.

16 Sherri Mitchell, *Sacred Instructions: Indigenous Wisdom for Living Spirit-Based Change* (Berkeley: North Atlantic Books, 2018), 57, 66–67.

17 Andrew Curry, "Parents' Emotional Trauma May Change Their Children's Biology. Studies in Mice Show How," *Science*, July 18, 2019, https://www.sciencemag.org/news/2019/07/parents-emotional-trauma-may-change-their-children-s-biology-studies-mice-show-how.

18 Wolynn, *It Didn't Start*, 25–26.

19 Heather Marcoux, "It's Science: Your Baby Will Always Be a Part of You," Motherly, December 5, 2017, https://www.mother.ly/its-science-your-baby-will-always-be-a-part-of-you.

20 "Everything You Ever Wanted to Know about the Rosetta Stone," *British Museum* (blog), July 14, 2017, https://blog.britishmuseum.org/everything-you-ever-wanted-to-know-about-the-rosetta-stone/.

Chapter 5

1 The names and some identifying details of this story have been changed.

2 Writer Drew Larson defines spiritual warfare as "the leveraging of everything that God promises against everything that opposes God's purposes. . . . Scripture tells us that there are real, actual spiritual forces arrayed against the triune God and his every goal, among which are your continued faithfulness and allegiance to Jesus." "What Spiritual Warfare Is (and What It Definitely Isn't)," *InterVarsity* (blog), November 13, 2015, https://intervarsity.org/blog/what-spiritual-warfare-and-what-it-definitely-isn-t. Satan and his demons are real, and a number of passages in Scripture highlight the ongoing battle in which believers find themselves. A few of these include Genesis 3:1; Job 1; Matthew 4:1–11; 2 Corinthians 10:4; Ephesians 6:10–18; Revelation 12:7–9.

3 Other relevant passages that point to generational consequences include Genesis 12:3; Exodus 34:6–7; Deuteronomy 5:9, 7:9; 24:16; Ezekiel 18:20; Daniel 9:16; John 9:1–3.

4 "The Sins of Our Fathers," Bible Project, accessed May 5, 2021, https://bibleproject.com/blog/the-sins-of-our-fathers/.

5 "Sins of Our Fathers."

6 Arah Iloabugichukwu, "Don't Confuse Generational Curses with Poor Generational Choices," Human Parts, December 11, 2019, https://humanparts.medium.com/dont-confuse-generational-curses-with-poor-generational-choices-a9c0590e012b.

7 Salient scripture passages referencing vows are found in Numbers 6; 30; Leviticus 22:21–23; 27; Deuteronomy 12:26; 23:21–25; Judges 11; 1 Samuel 1:11, 21; Job 22:27; Ecclesiastes 5:1–6; Matthew 5:33–37; Acts 18:18.

8 Arelene Lageson, "What Are Inner Vows and How Can They Be Broken?," *Walk Whole* (blog), July 8, 2017, https://walkwhole.com/2017/07/08/what-are-inner-vows-and-how-can-they-be-broken/.

9 Michelle Van Loon, *If Only: Letting Go of Regret* (Kansas City, MO: Beacon Hill, 2014), 116.

Chapter 6

1 The names and some identifying details of this story have been changed.

2 See "Adam Levine Sets Up Gwen Stefani & Blake Shelton," T-Mobile Big Game 2021 Commercial, February 7, 2021, https://www.youtube.com/watch?v=HxllNfjYw2U.

3 "Negative Space in Design: What It Is and Why It Matters," Framer Design Dictionary, accessed June 11, 2021, https://www.framer.com/dictionary/negative-space/.

4 Sophie Kay, "Negative Space: Making Your Genealogy Gaps Work For You (and Your Family Tree)," *The Parchment Rustler* (blog), accessed June 11, 2012, https://parchmentrustler.com/family-history/negative-space/.

5 Teresa Bonner, "Here's How the American Family Has Changed in the Past 50 Years," *PennLive Patriot-News*, last modified September 26, 2019, https://www.pennlive.com/news/erry-2018/06/3dd6bfa9da3775/heres_how_the_american_family.html.

6 U.S. Census Bureau, "Children under 18 Living with One Parent," November 12, 2020, https://www.census.gov/library/visualizations/2020/comm/children-under-18-living-with-one-parent.html.

7 Pew Research Center, "The American Family Today," December 17, 2015, https://www.pewresearch.org/social-trends/2015/12/17/1-the-american-family-today/.

8 Elizabeth Bernstein, "How Long Does It Take to Unite a Stepfamily?," *Wall Street Journal*, January 25, 2016, https://www.wsj.com/articles/how-long-does-it-take-for-a-stepfamily-to-gel-1453754797.

9 See "Wars since 1900," The Polynational War Memorial, accessed June 8, 2021, https://www.war-memorial.net/wars_all.asp.

10 Zhaoyang Liu, "Pogroms and Russian Jewish Immigrants," Re-Imagining Migration, last modified May 19, 2020, https://reimaginingmigration.org/pogroms-and-russian-jewish-immigrants/.

11 UNHCR Global Trends 2020, "Figures at a Glance," UNHCR,

June 18, 2021, https://www.unhcr.org/en-us/figures-at-a
-glance.html.

12 Rafael Bernal, "Biden Administration Identifies Almost 4,000
Migrant Children Separated during Trump Era," *The Hill*,
June 8, 2021, https://thehill.com/latino/557274-biden
-administration-identifies-almost-4000-migrant-children
-separated-during-trump.

13 Aishvarya Kavi, "A Court Filing Says Parents of 445 Separated
Migrant Children Still Have Not Been Found," *New York Times*,
April 7, 2021, https://www.nytimes.com/2021/04/07/us/
migrant-children-separated-border.html.

14 Zahirah McNatt et al., *Impact of Separation on Refugee Families:
Syrian Refugees in Jordan* (Amman: UNHCR, 2018), https://
data2.unhcr.org/en/documents/details/63840.

15 Abby Sewell, "Torn Apart by the Syrian War, These Siblings
Struggle to Stay Connected across 6 Different Countries," *The
World*, June 19, 2019, https://www.pri.org/stories/2019-06-19/
torn-apart-syrian-war-these-siblings-struggle-stay-connected
-across-6-different.

16 First Chronicles 3 offers a list of many of David's descendants.
Second Chronicles 11:18 also mentions Jerimoth as a son of
David not named in 1 Chronicles 3.

17 Peterborough Victoria Northumberland and Clarington Catholic District School Board, "Prayer for the Family," PVNCC,
February 2019, https://www.pvnccdsb.on.ca/wp-content/
uploads/2019/02/PrayerfortheFamily.pdf.

Chapter 7

1 Desmond Tutu, *God Has a Dream: A Vision of Hope for Our
Time* (New York: Image/Doubleday, 2005), 22.

2 Virginia Spence, "What Is the Adoption Rate?," Gladney Center for Adoption, September 23, 2018, https://adoption.org/
what-is-the-adoption-rate.

3 Bible Dictionary, s.v. "Adoption," Bible Study Tools, accessed
October 27, 2021, https://www.biblestudytools.com/dictionary/

adoption/. Verses include Romans 8:14–17, 23; 9:3–5; Galatians 4:4–7; Ephesians 1:4–6.

4   "Adoption History in Brief," Adoption History Project, February 24, 2012, https://darkwing.uoregon.edu/~adoption/topics/adoptionhistbrief.htm.

5   "Transracial Adoption," *Adoption Triad*, March 2019, https://www.childwelfare.gov/news-events/adoptiontriad/editions/mar2019/.

6   "Transracial Adoption."

7   Elizabeth J. Samuels, "How Adoption in America Grew Secret," October 21, 2001, https://www.washingtonpost.com/archive/opinions/2001/10/21/how-adoption-in-america-grew-secret/46b8a428-7e49-45d7-a0fc-cf13fd759b91/.

8   "US Adoption Statistics," Adoption Network, October 13, 2020, https://adoptionnetwork.com/adoption-myths-facts/domestic-us-statistics/.

9   Sharon Kaplan Roszia and Allison Davis Maxon, "Seven Core Issues in Adoption and Permanency," *Adoptalk*, no. 2 (August 15, 2019), https://www.nacac.org/resource/seven-core-issues-in-adoption-and-permanency/.

10 Sharon Vandivere, Karin Malm, and Laura Radel, *Adoption USA. A Chartbook Based on the 2007 National Survey of Adoptive Parents* (Washington, DC: U.S. Department of Health and Human Services, Office of the Assistant Secretary for Planning and Evaluation, 2009), https://aspe.hhs.gov/reports/adoption-usa-chartbook-based-2007-national-survey-adoptive-parents.

11 Mayo Clinic Staff, "Reactive Attachment Disorder," Mayo Clinic, July 13, 2017, https://www.mayoclinic.org/diseases-conditions/reactive-attachment-disorder/symptoms-causes/syc-20352939.

12 Not their real names; they are a composite of three sets of families I've known where the parents of older children adopted internationally are now dealing with that child's diagnosis of reactive attachment disorder.

13 The names and some identifying details in this story have been changed.

14 In addition, this commandment is referenced six places in the New Testament: Matthew 15:4; 19:19; Mark 7:10; 10:19; Luke 18:20; Ephesians 6:2.

15 John J. Parsons, "The Fifth Commandment," Hebrew for Christians, accessed June 30, 2021, https://www.hebrew4christians .com/Scripture/Torah/Ten_Cmds/Fifth_Cmd/fifth_cmd.html; *The NAS Old Testament Hebrew Lexicon*, s.v. "Kabed," Bible Study Tools, accessed June 30, 2021, https://www.biblestudytools .com/lexicons/hebrew/nas/kabed.html.

16 Kimberly Powell, "How to Handle Adoption in the Family Tree," ThoughtCo, last modified January 28, 2019, https://www .thoughtco.com/handling-adoption-in-the-family-tree -1421622.

Chapter 8

1 Quoted in Emma Bryce, "What's the Difference between Race and Ethnicity?," Live Science, February 8, 2020, https://www .livescience.com/difference-between-race-ethnicity.html.

2 Frederick Leong, *Encyclopedia of Counseling*, vol. 2 (Newbury Park, CA: Sage Publications, 2008), 1135.

3 Quoted in Larry Ferlazzo, "Saying 'I Don't See Color' Denies the Racial Identity of Students," *Education Week*, February 2, 2020, https://www.edweek.org/teaching-learning/opinion -saying-i-dont-see-color-denies-the-racial-identity-of-students/ 2020/02.

4 JaeRan Kim, "The Personal Is Political: Racial Identity and Racial Justice in Transracial Adoption," *Adoptalk*, no. 3 (November 5, 2018), https://www.nacac.org/resource/the-personal -is-political-racial-identity-and-racial-justice-in-transracial -adoption/.

5 "Population Distribution by Race, Ethnicity," Kaiser Family Foundation, last modified October 28, 2020, https://www.kff .org/other/state-indicator/distribution-by-raceethnicity; Iman Ghosh, "Visualizing U.S. Population by Race," Visual Capitalist, December 28, 2020, https://www.visualcapitalist.com/ visualizing-u-s-population-by-race/.

6   Dudley L. Poston Jr., "Three Ways That the U.S. Population Will Change over the Next Decade," *News Hour*, January 2, 2020, https://www.pbs.org/newshour/nation/3-ways-that-the-u-s -population-will-change-over-the-next-decade.

7   Over 90 percent of the Jewish population in the United States is Ashkenazi, that is, descendant of Jews who migrated north into eastern Europe and far western Asia in the centuries after the fall of the temple in AD 70. Other significant groupings of diaspora world Jewry include Sephardi Jews (those who migrated into North Africa and western Europe), Mizrahi Jews (often conflated with Sephardi Jews, this group moved into Arab Middle Eastern countries), and a handful of smaller diaspora communities concentrated in places like Ethiopia and India. According to the Spertus Institute for Jewish Learning and Leadership, 0.002 (two per thousand) or about 1 in every 480 people in the world are Jews. Byron L. Sherwin, "World Jewish Community," Spertus, accessed October 23, 2021, https://www .spertus.edu/subject-guides/sherwin-world-jewish-community.

8   A quinceañera is coming-of-age celebration for fifteen-year-old young women common in Mexico, parts of the United States, and some Central American countries.

9   Jean S. Phinney, "The Multigroup Ethnic Identity Measure: A New Scale for Use with Diverse Groups," *Journal of Adolescent Research* 7, no. 2 (April 1, 1992): 156–76, https://doi.org/ 10.1177/074355489272003, as cited in Allan Eason, "Ethnic Identity Development," Kansas State University, accessed July 5, 2021, https://tilford.k-state.edu/resources/ethnic-identity -development.html.

10 Wikipedia, s.v. "Religious Identity," last modified June 24, 2021, https://en.wikipedia.org/wiki/Religious_identity. While I don't love quoting from Wikipedia, these two sentences offer a really clear summary.

11 "The World Watch List," Open Door USA, August 23, 2021, https://www.opendoorsusa.org/christian-persecution/world -watch-list.

12 David Garrison, "Why More Muslims Are Turning to Jesus," *Newsweek*, June 28, 2019, https://www.newsweek.com/

christianity-islam-turning-jesus-1446327.

13 Judaism, Islam, and Christianity are monotheistic faiths; that is, they believe in one God. Christianity's distinctive is that this monotheism is expressed in the Trinity—one God in three persons, Father, Son, and Holy Spirit.

14 My religious identity formed from my faith in Jesus would not have saved me from Hitler's gas chambers, because my racial identity is Jewish.

15 Edward L. Queen II, "The Formation and Reformation of Religious Identity," Boston College, last modified September 26, 2021, https://www.bc.edu/content/dam/files/research_sites/cjl/sites/partners/erpp/CJC_Queen.htm.

16 The names and some identifying details of this story have been changed.

17 "Number of Single-Person Households U.S. 1960–2020," Statistica, May 18, 2021, https://www.statista.com/statistics/242022/number-of-single-person-households-in-the-us/.

18 *Shall We Dance?*, directed by Peter Chelsom (Los Angeles: Miramax, 2004).

19 John Donne, "Meditation XVII," *Devotions upon Emergent Occasions* (Cambridge, [UK]:The University Press, 1923. First published 1624.

Chapter 9

1 Greg Milo, *Rebooting Social Studies: Strategies for Reimagining History Classes* (New York: Rowman and Littlefield, 2017), 13.

2 Leslie Leyland Fields, *Your Story Matters: Finding, Writing, and Living the Truth of Your Life* (Colorado Springs, CO: NavPress, 2020), 41.

3 *Shtisel*, season 3, episode 9, "Where Does Everyone Suddenly Go?," directed by Alon Zingman, released February 14, 2021. One of the lead characters, Shulem Shtisel, is referring to an idea presented in Isaac Bashevis Singer's 1978 book *Shosha*, though it is not a direct quote from the book.

4 Matthew Fox, *Julian of Norwich: Wisdom in a Time of*

Pandemic—and Beyond (Bloomington, IN: iUniverse.com, 2020), conclusion.

5   Nancy Colier, "What Is Forgiveness and How Do You Do It?," *Psychology Today*, March 15, 2018, https://www.psychologytoday.com/us/blog/inviting-monkey-tea/201803/what-is-forgiveness-and-how-do-you-do-it.

6   "What Did Jesus Mean When He Said That We Should Forgive Others Seventy Times Seven?," Got Questions, July 19, 2011, https://www.gotquestions.org/seventy-times-seven.html.

7   Henri Nouwen, "Forgiveness," August 30, 2021, https://henrinouwen.org/meditation/forgiveness/.

8   Lewis B. Smedes, *The Art of Forgiving: When You Need to Forgive and Don't Know* (New York: Ballatine/Random House, 1996) 171.

9   A longer version of this account was first published on my blog: "Translating the Past," *Transforming Words* (blog), May 21, 2020, https://michellevanloon.com/2020/05/21/translating_the_past/.

10 *Finding Your Roots*, season 7, episode 5, "Write My Name in the Book of Life," directed by Jesse Sweet and Hazel Gurland, written by Henry Louis Gates Jr., featuring Pharrell Williams and Kasi Lemmons, aired February 16, 2021, on PBS.

11 "The WPA and the Slave Narrative Collection," Library of Congress, accessed October 21, 2021, https://www.loc.gov/collections/slave-narratives-from-the-federal-writers-project-1936-to-1938/articles-and-essays/introduction-to-the-wpa-slave-narratives/wpa-and-the-slave-narrative-collection/.

12 These words are broadly attributed to Philip Carr-Gomm, but I was unable to confirm the original source.

Appendix A

1   Ranier Maria Rilke, *Letters to a Young Poet* (Novato, CA: New World Library, 2000), 35.

2   Casey Tygrett, *Becoming Curious: A Spiritual Practice of Asking Questions* (Downers Grove, IL: InterVarsity Press, 2017), 26.

3   Bessel van der Kolk, *The Body Keeps the Score: Brain, Mind, and Body in the Healing of Trauma* (New York: Penguin Books, 2014), 1.

Appendix B

1   "What Is a Spiritual Director?," Diocese of St. Albans, last modified June 6, 2014, https://www.stalbans.anglican.org/ministry/what-is-a-spiritual-director.

The Author

SINCE SHE CAME TO FAITH in Christ at the tail end of the Jesus Movement, Michelle Van Loon's Jewish heritage, spiritual hunger, and storyteller's sensibilities have shaped her faith journey and informed her writing. Michelle has been a regular contributor at *Christianity Today* and *In Touch* magazines and has a wide range of published work, including curriculum, devotionals, articles, and plays. She is a founding member of the Pelican Project, a women's theology organization, and the cofounder of ThePerennialGen.com, a website for midlife women and men.

Michelle was on staff for five years at Trinity International University and earned a graduate certificate from Northern Seminary. She served as communications director for the former Christ Together Chicago, an organization that linked over seventy evangelical congregations across the north and northwest suburbs of the city in local mission. She served for nearly a decade as the U.S. administrator for the Caspari Center, a discipleship ministry based in Jerusalem.

   She was born in Chicago and lived in the Midwest until 2019, when she and her husband Bill relocated to Sarasota, Florida. (She misses family and friends, but not the cold weather!) Michelle and Bill have been married for more than forty years. They are parents of three and have two teenage grandsons. Michelle has been interested in family stories since the miniseries *Roots* first aired on television in 1977. Learn more about her writing and speaking ministry by visiting her website, MichelleVanLoon.com.